THE TEACHER'S GUIDE FOR THE NEW YORK STATE FOREIGN LANGUAGE PROFICIENCY EXAM WITH WRITING PREPARATION

Authors:
Rosemary L. Haigh
Patricia A. Lennon
Douglas E. Moore
Ellen Seidner
Nancy E. Wallace

Consultants:
Michelle Shenton-Mong
Carmela Taliercio-Cohn
Dr. Louise P. Terry
Marc Hobson
Walter Kleinmann

ISBN 978-1-879279-39-1

Proficiency Press Co.

Foreign Language Books by Master Teachers for Master Teachers

18 Lucille Avenue
Elmont, NY 11003

Phone/Fax (516) 775-0663
Toll Free 1-888-744-8363

Books Published By PROFICIENCY PRESS

Internet Tasks for Second Language Students (All Languages)
The Foreign Language Teacher's Handbook: *Aiming for Proficiency in French*, Second Edition
The Foreign Language Teacher's Handbook: *Aiming for Proficiency in German*, Second Edition
The Foreign Language Teacher's Handbook: *Aiming for Proficiency in Italian*, Second Edition
The Foreign Language Teacher's Handbook: *Aiming for Proficiency in Spanish*, Second Edition
The Foreign Language Teacher's Handbook *in Spanish* – Versions 2 & 3 (Book)
The Foreign Language Teacher's Handbook *in Spanish* – Versions 2 & 3 (CD)
The Teacher's Guide for the Updated N.Y.S. Foreign Language Proficiency Exam
Portfolio Assessment Tasks for the Beginning Level (All Languages)
Authentic Assessment for the Intermediate Level in French
Authentic Assessment for the Intermediate Level in Spanish
The Writing Tasks Guide for the Updated N.Y.S. Regents Exam (for Languages Other Than English)
C'est Ton Tour, *Aiming for Proficiency in French*, Second Edition
Dos Pasos Adelante
Du Bist Dran, *Aiming for Proficiency in German*
Te Toca A Ti, *Aiming for Proficiency in Spanish*, Second Edition
Te Toca A Ti, (Spanish) *Listening Comprehension CD*
Tocca A Te, *Aiming for Proficiency in Italian*, Second Edition
Tocca A Te, (Italian) *Listening Comprehension CD*
Suivez-moi, *Aiming for Proficiency in French*
Seguimi, *Aiming for Proficiency in Italian*
Sígueme, *Aiming for Proficiency in Spanish*
¡Hola! ¡Soy Yo!
Salut! C'est Moi!
Ciao! Sono Io!
Hallo! Hier Bin Ich!

**THE TEACHER'S GUIDE FOR THE NEW YORK STATE
FOREIGN LANGUAGE PROFICIENCY EXAM
WITH WRITING PREPARATION**
COPYRIGHT © 2008 by Proficiency Press
Printed in the United States

Camera-ready typing and layout of this manuscript by Michelle Shenton-Mong.
Cover design by Carmela Taliercio-Cohn.

PROFICIENCY PRESS CO.
18 Lucille Avenue, Elmont, New York 11003

ISBN 978-1-879279-39-1

ABOUT THE AUTHORS

Mrs. Rosemary Haigh (BA and MA French; Fulbright Scholar; graduate work at the Sorbonne, France; French Government Assistantship; American Association of Teachers of French National Secondary Teacher of the Year; National Honoree in the Walt Disney Salute to the American Teacher Program) Mrs. Haigh has taught in France, Poland, Australia and in Sewanhaka Central High School District, where she was honored as Teacher of the Year. Certified to teach French from pre-K through the advanced placement levels, Mrs. Haigh has co-authored several Proficiency Press publications. She is a past president of AATF, Nassau County.

Ms. Patricia Lennon (BA and MA in Spanish; Sewanhaka Central High School District Teacher of the Year; AATSP scholarship recipient; finalist as NYS Teacher of the Year; Embassy of Spain Scholarship, Salamanca, Spain) Ms. Lennon is Sewanhaka Central High School District Foreign Language Coordinator and an Adelphi University adjunct lecturer. A teacher of Spanish and English as a Second Language, she has co-authored several Proficiency Press publications. She is a past president of AATSP, Long Island Chapter.

Mr. Douglas Moore (BA in Spanish, MA in Teaching of English as a Second Language; studies at the University of Valencia, Spain) Mr. Moore is Foreign Language Chairperson at Copiague Public School District. He was selected Walt Whitman High School Teacher of the Year. He wrote and piloted the Exploratory Language Program in French, Italian, Latin and Spanish for Jericho Public Schools. He was South Huntington UFSD Technology and Teacher Mentor. He has co-authored several Proficiency Press publications. Mr. Moore is a past treasurer of AATSP, Long Island Chapter.

Ms. Ellen Seidner (BA in French; MA in Secondary Education; graduate studies in France) Ms. Seidner also has Spanish and FLES certification. Ms. Seidner teaches French and Spanish in the Sewanhaka Central High School District, where she co-authored the district's "Curriculum Guide in French for Checkpoint C" and updated the "Curriculum Guide for Checkpoint B."

Ms. Nancy Wallace (BA in French and Education; EdM in Foreign Language Education; graduate studies at Rutgers; Université de Toulouse, France, Université Laval; Québec; AATF Scholarship, Université d'Avignon, France; recipient of the Ferdinand DiBartolo Distinguished Service Award and the Ruth E. Wasley Distinguished Post Secondary Teacher Award from NYSAFLT; the Maryalice Seagrave Award for Outstanding Foreign Language Teacher in Western NY from WNYFLEC; and both the Distinguished Alumni Award and the Exemplary Service Award from the Graduate School of Education at Buffalo) Ms. Wallace has taught French and Spanish and was Instructional Leader of Foreign Language Department at Orchard Park Middle School. She also taught teacher education courses for both elementary and secondary levels at the University of Buffalo, St. Bonaventure University and State University College at Buffalo. She is a past president of NYSAFLT.

PREFACE

Expanded and revised, **The Teacher's Guide for the New York State Foreign Language Proficiency Exam with Writing Preparation** is designed for New York State world language teachers, as well as for all those interested in world language proficiency-driven methodology. Our book is written independently, by experienced New York State teachers for their colleagues.

Included in this useful teacher resource are:
- An overview of the N.Y.S. Proficiency exam
- Strategies for teaching the writing process
- Note-writing vocabulary and four function vocabulary in French, German, Italian and Spanish
- Topically arranged, reproducible writing tasks following the Proficiency Exam format
- Student writing task hints and practice rough draft writing sheet
- The N.Y.S. Syllabus
- Evaluation rubrics

The Teacher's Guide for the New York State Foreign Language Proficiency Exam with Writing Preparation is best used in conjunction with the Proficiency Press publication, **The Foreign Language Teacher's Handbook: *Aiming for Proficiency,*** available in French, German, Italian and Spanish. Together, these books form a complete program of topical assessment. Further ensuring student proficiency are the Proficiency Press language specific activity books, as well as portfolio and Internet books which provide student practice exercises.

This program, designed for use throughout the school year, provides an efficient means to focus on what is really needed for successful student foreign language proficiency.

TABLE OF CONTENTS

I. The New York State (N.Y.S.) Proficiency Exam   1

    ♦ Overview of the N.Y.S. Proficiency Exam   2

    ♦ Detailed Blueprint of the N.Y.S. Proficiency Exam   3

    ♦ The Proficiency Exam: Notes to the Teacher   6

II. Teaching Students to Write in the Target Language   7

    ♦ Hints for Teachers: Introducing Writing to Beginning
Foreign Language Students   8

    ♦ Activities to Aid Students with Spelling   11

    ♦ Teaching the Composition Writing Process   14

III. Useful Vocabulary   17

Note-writing, Socializing, Expressing Personal Feelings, Providing and Obtaining
Information, Persuading

    ♦ *French*   18

    ♦ *German*   25

    ♦ *Italian*   32

    ♦ *Spanish*   39

IV. Helpful Hints for Student Success on the N.Y.S. Proficiency Exam   47

    ♦ The Proficiency Exam Writing Section: Students' Helpful Hints   48

    ♦ Student Note-Writing Work Sheet   49

V. Student Writing Tasks   51

VI. Grading Criteria for Writing Tasks   79

VII. Grading Criteria for Informal and Formal Speaking   83

VIII. New York State Standards   91

ACKNOWLEDGMENT

We dedicate this book to our dear friend and Rosemary's beloved husband, Ian Haigh.

We would like to acknowledge those who have influenced our growth in proficiency methodology, Dr. Anthony Pappalia and Dr. Joseph Tursi, Sr.

We are grateful to the following people for their assistance in the creation and publication of this book: David Cohn, Sylvia Cohn, Noella Suzzi-Valli and Paulette White.

We would like to express our special appreciation to our families for their kind understanding and loving encouragement.

New York State Proficiency Exam

Overview of the N.Y.S. Proficiency Exam

Part 1A	Informal Speaking	10 points
Part 1B	Formal Speaking	20 points
Part 2A	Listening questions in English	20 points
Part 2B	Listening questions in the target language	10 points
Part 2C	Listening questions in picture form	10 points
Part 3A	Reading: 6 realia questions in English	12 points
Part 3B	Reading: 4 realia questions in the target language	8 points
Part 4	Writing ♦ 2 notes or other writing sample (e.g. journal entry) ♦ 30 words in target language	10 points
Total Points		100

Adapted from The New York State Standards

Detailed Blueprint of the N.Y.S. Proficiency Exam

I. __SPEAKING__   30 CREDITS

Part 1-A: 10 Credits for **INFORMAL SPEAKING**

Assessed in daily classroom activities, using rubrics and grading sheets (see pp. 85-89).

It is recommended that, in the beginning of the school year, teachers advise students and parents about the N.Y.S. Proficiency Exam's informal testing procedures and the rubrics used to evaluate student performance.

Part 1-B: 20 Credits for **FORMAL SPEAKING**

Formal Speaking Tasks are derived from the four functions and topics (see pp. 96-97). The tasks are distributed to schools in February.

Each student performs a total of four tasks. Each utterance receives 0 or 1 point. One point is given for quality*. There is a maximum of five points achieved for each of the four speaking tasks (see pp. 90-92).

---

*Guideline for the quality point:

For each task, students who require three or more second attempts **do not** qualify for the quality point. (Three or more check marks in the second column of the scoring sheet, make the student ineligible for the quality point.)

Responses eligible for the quality point contain evidence from each of the following categories as appropriate to Checkpoint A: Fluency, Complexity and Accuracy.

Detailed Blueprint of the N.Y.S. Proficiency Exam (con't)

II. <u>LISTENING COMPREHENSION</u>　　　　　40 CREDITS

This section consists of three parts. All questions are multiple choice.

Part 2-A: 20 Credits

Ten passages in the target language with student questions and answer choices in English.

Part 2-B: 10 Credits

Five passages in the target language with student questions and answer choices in the target language.

Part 2-C: 10 Credits

Five passages in the target language with student questions in English and picture answer choices.

III. <u>READING COMPREHENSION</u>　　　　　20 CREDITS

This section consists of two parts. All questions are multiple choice. Reading selections are realia based (ads, notices, notes, etc.).

Part 3-A: 12 Credits

Six student questions in English, each based on a target language reading selection.

Part 3-B: 8 Credits

Four student questions in the target language, each based on a target language reading selection.

Detailed Blueprint of the N.Y.S. Proficiency Exam (con't)

IV. <u>WRITING</u>   10 CREDITS

Part 4:

The Writing Tasks are derived from the four functions of language and the N.Y.S. topics (see pp. 96-103). Part 4 contains a choice of two out of three Writing Tasks.

Students must write a minimum of 30 words in the target language for each task in order to receive the full credit of 5 points for each task. The tasks most typically are informal notes, but may also include other writing samples, such as journal entries (see pp. 79-82).

**Part 4
Grading Criteria for Checkpoint A**

Read each note to determine:

- if the **purpose** has been achieved
- the level of **vocabulary** used
- the type of **structure** exhibited
- the **Word count**: There must be **30** words. A word is a letter or collection of letters, surrounded by space, that is in the target language, is comprehensible, and contributes to the development of the task.

  - Do not count names of people.
  - Do not count places and brand names not in the target language.
  - Contractions are counted as one word.
  - Salutations and closings are counted.
  - Abbreviations in the target language are counted.
  - Grammatically incorrect words can count. For example, in Spanish *de el* (*del*) count as two words.

The Proficiency Exam: Notes to the Teacher

1) In the beginning of the school year, decide on your **informal speaking strategy** (see p. 3) and communicate it, as well as evaluation rubrics, to students and parents.

2) It is important to identify **students with special needs** and refer to their I.E.P. at the beginning of the school year. Spelling exemptions may be allowed if so stated in the I.E.P. Foreign Language teachers must apprise themselves of N.Y.S. Proficiency Exam regulations regarding students with disabilities, communicate early with school officials about special testing/grading procedures, and see that they are carried out.

3) Students whose **religious beliefs** require substitute tasks during the school year similarly are eligible for substitute tasks on the Proficiency Exam.

4) A student may be eligible to receive N.Y.S. Foreign Language credit for participation in **bilingual education programs** or credit for **education and residence in an other-than-English-speaking environment**. Refer to N.Y.S. Education Department guidelines. See *Questions and Answers Policy* sheet at http://www.emsc.nysed.gov/ciai/lote/.

5) With administrator approval a student may be allowed to **challenge the N.Y.S. Proficiency Exam**, if the student satisfactorily completes a project reflecting classroom learning activities, and receives a score of 85% or above on the exam.

6) **Examination scoring information** is available at the N.Y.S. Education Department's website: http://www.emsc.nysed.gov/osa/. It is recommended to visit this website during the rating period and before final exam scores are recorded.

7) Although the Proficiency Exam contains no separate target language culture part, **culture is embedded** in questions throughout the exam.

8) As soon as possible in the school year, **include test questions in the format of the Proficiency Exam** in your student assessments so that test question format will not be a negative factor in student performance on the N.Y.S. Proficiency Exam.

Teaching Students to Write in the Target Language

HINTS FOR TEACHERS: INTRODUCING WRITING TO BEGINNING FOREIGN LANGUAGE STUDENTS

In order to prepare students for successful composition writing a variety of pre-writing activities, progressing from simple to more complex, is recommended. Suggestions include:

♦ students **COPY** key vocabulary words or short phrases from the current topic into their notebooks.

♦ students **LABEL** pictures of vocabulary words. This activity is most effective when the picture illustrates a setting in which the words would typically be used. For example, students label the fruit in a picture of the fruit stand at the market or classroom objects in a picture of a classroom.

♦ students **MAKE FLASHCARDS** of new vocabulary with a picture or drawing of the word on one side and the word in the target language on the other side.

♦ students **SUPPLY THE MISSING LETTERS** (or just missing vowels) in a list of words from the current topic. For example, for the clothing unit, a list might include:

   the sw___ ___ t ___ r   and the j ___ ck ___t

Students fill in the missing letters and then copy over the complete words *the sweater and the jacket*. Students can then use these words to label a picture of clothing items.

♦ students **UNSCRAMBLE** vocabulary words and rewrite them correctly. For example, for a unit on school, students unscramble the word **otokebon** to form the word *notebook*. As they advance, they may be asked to use the unscrambled word to label a picture or to write a simple sentence.

♦ students **WRITE LISTS** of vocabulary words that they have already learned that relate to a specific theme. For example, students are told "You are going on a picnic. Make a list of items you plan to bring." Students may do this in class, alone or with a partner, or as a homework assignment or a journal entry. This is also a helpful step in brainstorming ideas for a composition.

♦ students **COMPLETE FORMS** with appropriate information. Hotel registration forms, customs forms and order forms work well.

♦ students **FILL IN THE BLANKS** with appropriate vocabulary words. For example, students complete a sentence, then copy over the entire sentence.

sentence:	For lunch, I eat _____ and _____.
student fills in:	For lunch, I eat *a sandwich* and *an apple*.
student copies over:	For lunch, I eat a sandwich and an apple.

♦ As they advance, students engage in **GUIDED WRITING.** In the sample below, they use a form letter with blanks for personal information to assist them in writing their first pen pal or e-pal letter. For example:

Dear _____,
   My name is _____. *I am* _____ *years old. I live in* _____. *I have* _____*brothers and* _____*sisters. My favorite sport is* _____.   *(etc.)*

The completed form can be checked over by the teacher or a student partner. The letter is then copied over onto stationery or word processed for e-mail.

♦ In a similar activity, students are asked to create a fantasy animal by combining the traits of several different animals. The teacher gives them the form below to fill out in which they name their creature and describe its characteristics. They then copy over the information and draw a picture of their animal.

My animal is a _____.
It has the _____ of a _____.
It has the _____ of a _____.
It is _____ and _____. (adjectives)
It likes to _____ and _____.
It does not like to _____.

In another variation of this activity, students are asked to create and write a guided paragraph about a monster, naming it, telling the number of heads, eyes, toes, etc., that it has and then illustrating their monster.

♦ students read a short passage in the target language, then **SUMMARIZE** or **RETELL** the information. For example,

Students read:
   My name is Pepe. I am 13 years old. I live in Granada, Spain. My favorite sport is soccer.

Students write:
   His name is Pepe. He is 13 years old. He lives in Granada, Spain. His favorite sport is soccer.

♦ students **USE THE INTERNET** at a site pre-screened by the teacher to gather information to complete a worksheet. A reliable source for such activities is the Proficiency Press book entitled *Internet Tasks for Second Language Students* by David Cohn, Douglas E. Moore and Carmela Taliercio-Cohn.

♦ students keep a **JOURNAL** or **PERSONAL DIARY** in the target language making entries several times a week following teacher directions. Entries can be as simple as making a list of needed school supplies or more complex expressing their feelings about an event. These entries can be the beginning of the brainstorming process in preparation for writing a composition.

♦ students **ANSWER SIMPLE QUESTIONS** in complete sentences beginning with yes or no answers and progressing to questions requiring students to supply appropriate information. For example:

Question:	Do you like spinach?
Student answer:	Yes, I like spinach. or No, I do not like spinach.
Question:	At what time does the movie begin?
Student answer:	The movie begins at 7:30.

♦ students **COMPLETE SUBSTITUTION DRILLS.** For example:

	Paul is going to the library.
	(bank) _____
Student writes:	Paul is going to the bank.
	(café) _____
Student writes:	Paul is going to the café.

♦ students are given a series of individual words on the chalkboard, overhead or on pieces of paper in an envelope. They are to **PUT THE WORDS IN ORDER** to make a meaningful sentence, then copy the complete sentence into their notebooks. For example: students are given the following words:

station the Paris for 13.30 leaves train the at

Students re-arrange the words to form the sentence "The train for Paris leaves the station at 13.30." The correct sentence is copied into notebooks. This activity is most effective if a series of 3 or 4 topically connected sentences are re-arranged and copied over to form a cohesive paragraph.

♦ students **EXPAND SENTENCES** by participating with the class in sentence build-up activities. For example, the teacher writes the word "shirt" on the chalkboard or overhead. Students take turns adding a word until no one can come up additional words that make sense.

	SHIRT
Student 1 adds the	the shirt
Student 2 adds blue	the blue shirt
Student 3 adds is	the blue shirt is
Student 4 adds ugly	the blue shirt is ugly
Student 5 adds very	The blue shirt is very ugly.

This activity can also be done as a contest with partners to see which pair in the class can create the longest sentence. Many students enjoy being asked to come up with the starter word.

ACTIVITIES TO AID STUDENTS WITH SPELLING

Spelling in the target language is a skill Checkpoint A students can master even if spelling is not a strength in their first language. Their age and maturity, a fresh start with a brand new language plus a systematic approach to spelling can lead to successful skill development. Helpful activities include:

♦ teacher practices with the class the letters of the **ALPHABET** in the target language until students can recite the complete alphabet correctly.

♦ teacher chooses 5 to 8 **KEY WORDS** or 2 to 3 **KEY EXPRESSIONS** for the week. These words or expressions are chosen for utility and frequency as aids in student writing. Longer lists can be overwhelming and can cause some students to give up without trying. They are most effective when centered around a common theme or topic. Students are expected to copy over and practice spelling the words or expressions during the week, learning the correct spelling in preparation for a quiz at the end of the week.

♦ teacher chooses a **WORD OF THE WEEK**. Every time anyone says that word, the class stops, repeats the word, spells the word in the target language and repeats the word again before returning to their work.

♦ teacher gives students a written list of current vocabulary words and asks them to **ALPHABETIZE** the words and then copy over the alphabetized list.

♦ teacher gives a list of scrambled vocabulary words to a team or to partners. Their task is to **UNSCRAMBLE** the words and copy over the list, spelling each word correctly.

♦ teacher distributes picture bingo cards to students and then proceeds to play **SPELLING BINGO** in the usual fashion with the exception that, in order to win, a student must not only cover appropriate spaces but must also identify the pictures covered in the target language and spell the words correctly in the target language.

♦ teacher assigns **WORD SEARCH (WORD FIND) PUZZLES** in which students locate vocabulary words from the current topic, circle them within the puzzle and then copy them over. When all the words have been found and copied over, students check their spelling against their vocabulary list. If they have miscopied or misspelled a word, they are encouraged to copy the word correctly 3 times to reinforce the correct spelling. In the early stages, a word bank can be given but students are still required to copy over the words that they find within the puzzle. There are many software programs available that will create puzzles from the words supplied by the teacher.

♦ teacher assigns a **CROSSWORD PUZZLE** utilizing current vocabulary. The clues can either be pictures or fill-in the blank sentences in which students first complete the sentence with the missing word and then write that word in the appropriate spot in the puzzle. Again, there are software programs available that will create puzzles from the words supplied by the teacher.

♦ teacher gives students a key word around which they are to create a **WEB** with as many related words as they can come up with in a specified number of minutes. For example, the teacher starts the web with the word "breakfast". Students make a web around "breakfast" with words such as cereal, toast, orange juice, etc.

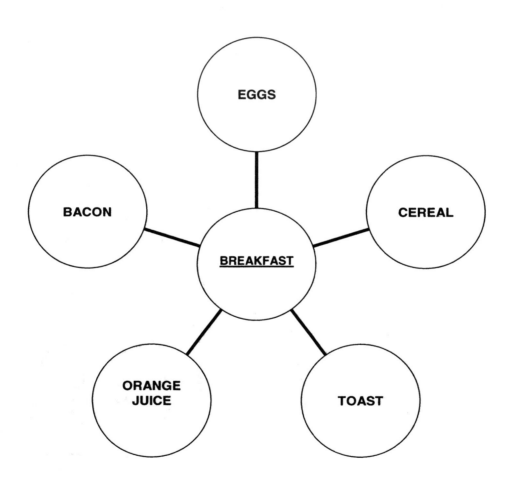

♦ teacher assigns students to create a **CONCRETE POEM** (using the word over and over again to form a picture of the word) or a **CALLIGRAM** (a word written to outline the shape of the object) or a **WORD PICTURE** (drawing an image of the word meaning within the letters of the word). When finished, the student may embellish the poem with color and appropriate additions.

CONCRETE POEM

CALLIGRAM

WORD PICTURES

TEACHING THE COMPOSITION WRITING PROCESS

Simple writing tasks in the target language can be intimidating and even overwhelming to beginning students. Although they are very familiar with the writing process from their English Language Arts (ELA) classes, they rarely automatically transfer those skills to their new language. Therefore, it is important to show them how to apply the same strategies in the target language.

Although the ultimate goal for Checkpoint A students is to write a 30 word composition following the rubrics of the New York State Proficiency Examination as a guide, their initial attempts at writing need to be carefully scaffolded.

In the very beginning stages there is no need to mention rubrics or to try for 30 words. To start writing:

- ◆ The teacher asks students, either individually or as a group, to brainstorm vocabulary in the target language that is pertinent to the topic assigned.
- ◆ Students copy the vocabulary into their writing notebook (or into a section of their regular notebook labeled writing).
- ◆ Then the teacher explains the task and asks students for suggestions on how to accomplish the task. As students make suggestions, the teacher writes them on the chalkboard or the overhead projector.
- ◆ The teacher helps students to organize their suggestions into a cohesive and comprehensible composition of about 12 words that accomplishes the task. Students then copy the composition into their writing notebooks.
- ◆ Students work together with the teacher to write 2 or 3 more similar compositions before they write their first one on their own. Students are taught to look for word count, subject/verb agreement, noun/adjective agreement, cohesiveness, logical progression of thought and accomplishment of task. They are also encouraged to use their notebooks and textbooks for support.

Once the students have experience writing simpler, shorter tasks, the teacher presents the rubric for the writing tasks on the NYS Proficiency Exam. Students put a copy of the rubric in their writing notebooks and take a copy of the rubric home to share with their parents.

Then, when students are ready to tackle longer compositions, the following process is used:

- careful **READING** of the task.

- **BRAINSTORM** appropriate vocabulary either as a group or as a homework assignment from the previous class.

- **DISCUSSION** of ways to accomplish the task, emphasizing that there are many ways to accomplish the task.

- students prepare a **FIRST DRAFT** written on every other line.

- students **SELF-CHECK** their own work to see if they have accomplished the task, if the composition makes sense, if they have written a sufficient number of words, if they have made subject/verb and adjective/noun agreements, etc.

- students share their first draft with a partner for **PEER REVIEW**. The partner checks the same items as in the self-check, making suggestions for improvement and signs the bottom of the draft for accountability.

- students write a **SECOND DRAFT** using suggestions from the peer reviewer, if desired, and submits the first and second drafts to the teacher.

- teacher **REVIEWS AND CORRECTS** the second draft according to the rubric and returns it to the student.

- using the teacher corrections, students **REWRITE** the composition. At this point, the composition can be placed in the student's writing **PORTFOLIO**. For suggestions on how to organize, implement and store portfolios in the foreign language classroom, consult the book *Portfolio Assessment Tasks for the Beginning Level* by Patricia Lennon and Douglas Moore, published by Proficiency Press.

The University of the State of New York
THE STATE EDUCATION DEPARTMENT
Albany, New York 12234

Regents Comprehensive Examinations in Modern Languages

Teacher's Manual for Administering and Scoring Part 1: Speaking

DET 555M (6-08—10,000)
98-14801

GENERAL INFORMATION

The Regents comprehensive examination in each modern language is designed to measure students' attainment of learning outcomes at Checkpoint B of the State syllabus *Modern Languages for Communication*. The examination includes 24 credits for oral communication performance in Part 1 and 76 credits for a written test of listening comprehension, reading comprehension, and writing skills.

Part 1 of the examination consists of a formal speaking test to be administered at the school's convenience during the speaking test period, *which begins ten weeks prior to the written test and ends five calendar days prior to the written test*. The 60 tasks in the speaking test for each January and June examination are to be selected by the school from the *Sourcebook of Speaking Tasks for Part 1* provided by the State Education Department. Specific information about the selection of the speaking tasks is provided below.

It is expected that students with certain disabilities use specialized/adaptive equipment and instruction/demonstration techniques during second language instruction. When taking the Regents examinations in modern languages, such students should be provided the same specialized/adaptive equipment and instruction/demonstration techniques, as well as the alternative testing techniques indicated in their Individualized Education Program. It is the responsibility of the principal to ensure that alternative testing techniques are provided to students with disabilities as recommended by the Committee on Special Education. In addition, when determining who should be tested, administrators must consider those students with disabilities who attend programs operated by the Board of Cooperative Educational Services (BOCES), as well as any other programs located outside the school.

The students' scores for Part 1 must be completed in ink and must be reported to the building principal *no later than five calendar days prior to the date of the written test*. A sample reporting sheet is provided on page 10.

THE SPEAKING TEST

Description

The speaking test consists of communication tasks to be performed by students with their teacher. Each task prescribes a simulated conversation in which the student always plays the role of himself/herself and the teacher assumes the specific role indicated in each task. The tasks may involve one or more of the four communication functions specified in the State syllabus: socializing, providing and obtaining information, expressing personal feelings or opinions, and getting others to adopt a course of action.

Each student performs a total of two tasks, randomly selected from the 60 speaking tasks comprising Part 1, as chosen by the school from the sourcebook. Each task consists of a brief statement in English to indicate the purpose and setting of the communication, the role of the teacher, and the person who is to initiate the conversation. Each task is designed so that it can be completed in six interactions between the student and the teacher. For the purpose of this manual, the student's part in each of these interactions is called an *utterance*.

Selection of the Part 1 Speaking Tasks

The State Education Department provides a collection of speaking tasks in the publication *Sourcebook of Speaking Tasks for Part 1*. The 60 speaking tasks that constitute Part 1 of a Regents comprehensive examination in a modern language are to be selected by the school from this sourcebook. Since the sourcebook will *not* be revised on an annual basis, it will serve as the source of the Part 1 speaking tests for current and future administrations of modern language examinations. **The sourcebook contains secure examination material and must be kept under lock and key when not in use.**

20 listen x 2 = 20

20 reading x 1 = 20

2 Writing x 5 = 10

Speaking

15 verbs

$\delta\!\!\!/$

(5) credits

* (Initialize

= more than 1 word
= use of verbs

I
II
III
IV }

Subtotal
" V " 15 sentences
verbs in banks

Speaking

WORD BANK

aller à la piscine
aller au café
aller au cinéma
la balle/le ballon
la batte
la bibliothèque
le centre commercial
danser
discuter (avec des amis)
faire du sport
faire la fête
faire les magasins (m.)
faire un pique-nique
jouer au base-ball/foot(ball)
jouer aux cartes/aux échecs
le lycée
la Maison des jeunes et de la Culture (MJC)
nager

park
stadium
to go out
to see a movie
Do you usually like to :...?
Yes, often.
From time to time.
No, rarely./No, never.

	Informal	Formal	1 April to	Sarah	only (B) (3) - in lycée is peak	You're stuck with this task ask questions before choosing
13. To go out						
14. To dance						
15. To chat (with friends)						
16. Stadium						
17. Recreation center						
18. Park						
19. No, rarely./No. never.						
20. Mall						
21. Library						
22. High school						
23. From time to time.						
24. Do you usually like to...?						
25. Bat						
26. Ball						

Speaking tasks for Part 1 of the January and June administrations of modern language examinations should be selected as early in the school year as possible. For each successive administration of the speaking test, a new set of 60 tasks must be selected. Each succeeding set of 60 speaking tasks should not have been used in the preceding administration of the speaking test. The selection of the speaking test tasks for the current school year must be made before students have the opportunity to practice with the remainder of the speaking tasks in the sourcebook. The principal should take all necessary precautions to ensure that the Part 1 speaking test tasks to be administered in January and in June of the current school year are kept secure.

The following procedures are recommended for selection of the Part 1 speaking test:

- Select the 60 speaking tasks from the sourcebook, taking care not to select any tasks that were used for the most recent administration of the examination.
- Make a photocopy of each page of the sourcebook containing any of the 60 tasks selected.
- Remove the 60 speaking tasks from the photocopied pages and mount them on index cards, one task per card.
- At the test administration, the student picks a card, hands it to the teacher, and the teacher reads the task aloud to the student.

OR

- Select the 60 speaking tasks from the sourcebook, taking care not to select any tasks that were used for the most recent administration of the examination.
- Renumber the selected tasks from 1 to 60. Also number small pieces of paper from 1 to 60 and place the numbered slips in a box.
- At the test administration, the student picks a numbered slip from the box and hands the slip to the teacher. The teacher locates the task in the sourcebook that corresponds to the number and reads the task aloud to the student.

For any given school year, the tasks not selected for Part 1 of a January or June examination may be used for instructional purposes. However, caution must be exercised to ensure that the complete set of printed speaking tasks in the sourcebook is kept secure at all times.

Administration and Rating

The speaking test is to be administered individually to each student at the school's convenience at any time during the speaking test period, either in the presence of other students or with only the teacher. The two tasks need not be administered to each student at one sitting; they may be administered one task at a time during the entire speaking test period. **The Part 1 speaking tasks must be kept secure from the time they are initially selected at the beginning of the school year to the end of the speaking test period.**

The student is to pick two tasks **at random** from the 60 speaking tasks previously selected to constitute Part 1. Depending on the administration method used by the teacher or school, the student will either:

- Pick an index card from the unnumbered group of 60 cards, hand it to the teacher, and the teacher will read the task aloud to the student.

OR

- Pick a numbered slip of paper from a box of 60 numbered slips and hand it to the teacher. The teacher will locate the task in the sourcebook that corresponds to the number and will read the task aloud to the student.

Once a task has been selected by the student, it cannot be substituted for another or done over if the first performance is unsatisfactory.* Care should be taken that no student selects the same task twice.

In administering the test, the teacher has two major responsibilities: (1) to act as the student's conversation partner, and (2) to rate the student's performance.

As the conversation partner, the teacher applies real-life communication devices in the target language to keep the student on task and to ensure the continuity of the conversation. Communication devices such as "Sorry, I didn't understand that," "Would you say that again, please," or "No, what I meant was..." could be used in the target language for that purpose. An additional responsibility of the teacher as the conversation partner is to help bring the conversation to a natural conclusion.

As the conversation partner, the teacher influences the student's performance by the nature of the eliciting attempts. In order to qualify for full credit, the student's utterances must be consistent with the breadth of content expected at Checkpoint B in the syllabus. Utterances that are comprehensible and appropriate but insufficient in content receive less than full credit. Very focused eliciting attempts may place students in situations where such responses are unavoidable. Questions that focus narrowly on "who," "when," "where," and "at what time," for example, tend to elicit very limited responses which, although perfectly natural, do not provide students the opportunity to demonstrate all they can do.

Whenever possible, eliciting attempts should be open-ended statements rather than questions. Whenever questions are unavoidable, they should be as open-ended as possible. Ideally, the teacher should say as little as is necessary to elicit maximum responses by students.

As conversation partner and rater, the teacher may make two attempts at eliciting any of the six student utterances. If the student has not produced a comprehensible and appropriate utterance after the teacher's first two eliciting attempts at the very beginning of the conversation, the student receives no credit for the entire task. However, during the conversation, if a student has not produced a comprehensible and appropriate utterance after the teacher's second eliciting attempt, the student receives no credit for that utterance, and the teacher should then shift to another aspect of the task.

To facilitate rating while acting as the conversation partner, the teacher should use a score sheet to keep track of the student's utterances, to record the number of eliciting attempts for each, and to record the number of credits awarded for each utterance. A sample score sheet is provided on page 11.

Certain teacher-student interactions, although natural in the course of a conversation, do not provide evidence of the student's ability to produce language. They should be disregarded for rating purposes. Examples of such interactions are:

- "yes/no" responses
- restatements of all or essential parts of what the teacher has said
- proper names used in isolation
- socializing devices ("Hello," "How are you," etc.) used in isolation [Note: socializing devices at the beginning of a conversation may serve the "initiating" purpose, but do not qualify for credit as an utterance.]

---

*At times, the task a student selects may not be appropriate for that student, usually due to a student's particular disability or religious beliefs. In such cases, that student should be allowed to substitute another task. In order for the student with the disability to be eligible to substitute a task, that student must have been identified by the school district's Committee on Special Education as having a disability, and the need for the substitution must be consistent with the student's Individualized Education Program (IEP). A student is eligible to substitute tasks due to religious beliefs if it can be demonstrated that the student has been excused from participating in similar conversational situations during the school year.

As the rater, the teacher gives a maximum of *12 credits* for each task according to the following criteria:

- Award 2 credits for each of the student's six utterances that is comprehensible, appropriate, and consistent with the following proficiency statement at Checkpoint B of the syllabus:

   "Can initiate and sustain a conversation, but limited vocabulary range necessitates hesitation and circumlocution. Can use the more common verb tense forms, but still makes many errors in formation and selection. Can use word order accurately in simple sentences, but still makes errors in more complex patterns. Can sustain coherent structures in short and familiar communicative situations. Can employ selectively basic cohesive features such as pronouns and verb inflections. Extended communication is largely a series of short, discrete utterances. Can articulate comprehensibly but has difficulty in producing certain sounds in certain positions or combinations. Speech is usually labored. Has to repeat to be understood by the general public."

   As used above, the term "comprehensibility" means that the utterance would make sense to native speakers who know no English, and the term "appropriateness" means that the utterance contributes to the completion of the task.

- Award 1 credit for each of the student's six utterances that is comprehensible and appropriate, but below the level indicated in the proficiency statement at Checkpoint B.

- Award 0 credit for utterances that are incomprehensible or inappropriate following the teacher's second eliciting attempt.

SAMPLE ADMINISTRATION OF A TASK

The student has randomly selected the following task:

---

25. [Teacher initiates] Teacher says: I am a student. You are an exchange student in my school. We have just heard that a school trip has been canceled. We are going to share our reactions to that decision. I will start the conversation.

PRESENTATION OF TASK

Teacher Says in English

I am a student. You are an exchange student in my school. We have just heard that a school trip has been canceled. We are going to share our reactions to that decision. I will start the conversation.* – Do you understand the situation?

All right. Remember that we'll be talking about a school trip that has been canceled. I'll give you a few seconds to think about what you may want to say in (target language) in this situation. (Short pause)

All right. Are you ready?

From now on, we'll use no more English.

Student Says in English

Yes, I think so.

Yes, I am.

TASK BEGINS (ALL IN TARGET LANGUAGE)

Teacher Says	Student Says	Rating
(1) Did you hear about Saturday's school trip?	No, I did not go.	Comprehensible but inappropriate. Student has one more opportunity for this utterance. Teacher should make second eliciting attempt.
No, no! I mean the trip to the play this coming weekend.	What is about it?	*1 credit:* Comprehensible and appropriate, but below Checkpoint B.
(2) It's been canceled.	It has been canceled?	Restatement: Disregard. Teacher should make first eliciting attempt again.
That's right. We're not going.	Is too bad. I bought new clothing for it.	*2 credits:* Comprehensible and appropriate, consistent with Checkpoint B.

---

* **NOTE:** The teacher reads the task aloud to the student **exactly as provided by the State Education Department.**

Teacher Says	Student Says	Rating
(3) Never mind about the clothes. What about the money we paid for the tickets!	What can we do?	*2 credits:* Comprehensible and appropriate, consistent with Checkpoint B.
(4) I think we should get a lot of kids to march to the office and demand our money!	No.	"Yes/no" response: Disregard. Teacher should make first eliciting attempt again.
Why not?	It not…ah…need… ah…necessary.	*1 credit:* Comprehensible and appropriate, but below Checkpoint B.
(5) You don't know them very well.	I think…ah, ah [unintelligible sounds]	Incomprehensible. Student has one more opportunity for this utterance. Teacher should make second eliciting attempt.
What did you say?	You know not.	*0 credit:* Second attempt is inappropriate. Teacher should make first eliciting attempt for utterance 6.
(6) I can't wait for them to give me my money back.	You mean too much money?	Comprehensible but inappropriate. Student has one more opportunity for this utterance. Teacher should make second eliciting attempt.
I need my money now!	If you needed money, I will lend it to you.	*2 credits:* Comprehensible and appropriate, consistent with Checkpoint B.
Good, thanks. I'll take you up on it.		

Task Ends

MODERN LANGUAGE REGENTS EXAMINATION
SAMPLE SCORE SHEET
PART 1: SPEAKING

Student's Name: _____Jane Doe_____

Language: _____Sample Task - English_____

	Utterance		First Attempt	Second Attempt
First Task: No. 25	1	(__) *	-	1
	2		2	
	3		2	
	4		1	
	5		-	0
	6		-	2

TOTAL: **8**

	Utterance		First Attempt	Second Attempt
Second Task: No. _____	1	(__) *		
	2			
	3			
	4			
	5			
	6			

TOTAL: _____

Use a checkmark to indicate student's initiation of the conversation, if required.

MODERN LANGUAGE REGENTS EXAMINATION
SAMPLE REPORTING SHEET
PART 1: SPEAKING

(To be completed in ink and submitted to the Principal's office at least 5 calendar days before the date of the written test)

STUDENT'S NAME	First Task (0-12)	Second Task (0-12)	TOTAL*

*This score is to be transferred to the student's answer booklet for the written test.

Language _____ Class Period _____ Teacher _____

School _____ City or P.O. _____

Received in my Office _____ _____

Date   Principal's signature

MODERN LANGUAGE REGENTS EXAMINATION
SAMPLE SCORE SHEET
PART 1: SPEAKING

Student's Name: _____

Language: _____

	Utterance		First Attempt	Second Attempt
First Task: No. _____	1	(__) *	_____	_____
	2		_____	_____
	3		_____	_____
	4		_____	_____
	5		_____	_____
	6		_____	_____

TOTAL: [   ]

Second Task: No. _____	1	(__) *	_____	_____
	2		_____	_____
	3		_____	_____
	4		_____	_____
	5		_____	_____
	6		_____	_____

TOTAL: [   ]

* Use a checkmark to indicate student's initiation of the conversation, if required.

The University of the State of New York
THE STATE EDUCATION DEPARTMENT
Albany, New York 12234

SECOND LANGUAGE PROFICIENCY EXAMINATIONS MODERN LANGUAGES

Teacher's Manual for Administering and Scoring Part 1: Speaking

> **Includes rubric for scoring Part 1a and guidelines for awarding Part 1b quality credit**

DET 1352 (3-05—20,000) 94-93628

OVERVIEW OF EXAMINATION

This overview provides a description of the Second Language Proficiency Examinations in Modern Languages. For additional information, refer to the publication *Second Language Proficiency Examination for Modern Languages: Test Changes and Sampler*, which is accessible on the Department's web site at http://www.emsc.nysed.gov/ciai/pub/publote.html.

SPEAKING

Part 1a
(10 credits)

Students' oral communication performance is assessed in daily classroom activities from April 1 until five calendar days prior to the date of the written examination. Teachers must use the Part 1a rubric to assess student performance. The rubric and guidelines for using the rubric are provided in this manual.

Part 1b
(20 credits)

Schools select 20 tasks for each of four language functions from the *Sourcebook of Speaking Tasks for Part 1* provided by the State Education Department. Each student chooses a total of four tasks. The tasks are to be administered from April 1 until five calendar days prior to the date of the written examination. This manual provides the guidelines for administering and rating Part 1b as well as the guidelines for awarding the quality credit.

LISTENING

Part 2a
(20 credits)

Ten multiple-choice questions measuring comprehension of oral target-language stimuli; responses provided in English

Part 2b
(10 credits)

Five multiple-choice questions measuring comprehension of oral target-language stimuli; responses provided in target language

Part 2c
(10 credits)

Five multiple-choice questions measuring comprehension of oral target-language stimuli; responses provided in the form of pictures

READING

Part 3a
(12 credits)

Six multiple-choice questions measuring comprehension of written target-language stimuli; responses provided in English

Part 3b
(8 credits)

Four multiple-choice questions measuring comprehension of written target-language stimuli; responses provided in target language

WRITING

Part 4
(10 credits)

Two writing tasks (chosen from three provided), each requiring a response of at least 30 words in the target language that satisfies the purpose of the task. Each task is worth a maximum of 5 credits. Tasks are scored using the writing rubric provided.

GENERAL INFORMATION

The proficiency examination in each modern language is designed to measure students' attainment of learning outcomes at Checkpoint A of the State syllabus *Modern Languages for Communication*. The examination includes 30 credits for oral communication performance in Part 1 and 70 credits for a written test of listening comprehension, reading comprehension, and writing skills. Part 1 of the examination consists of the following two subparts:

Part 1a:	Assessment of student performance in daily classroom activities during the period from April 1 until five calendar days prior to the date of the written test [10 credits]
	Beginning with the 2000–01 school year, you must use the rubric provided on page 12 of this manual to assess student performance on Part 1a. The rubric was developed to provide more guidance to scorers and to increase consistency in the scoring process across the State. Specific information about using the rubric is provided below.
Part 1b:	Formal speaking test to be administered at the school's convenience from April 1 until five calendar days prior to the date of the written test [20 credits]
	The school must select the 80 tasks in the speaking test for each June administration from the *Sourcebook of Speaking Tasks for Part 1* provided by the State Education Department. Specific information about the selection of the speaking tasks is provided below.
	Beginning with the 2000–01 school year, you must use new guidelines for awarding the quality credit. Specific information about awarding the quality credit is provided below.

You must report the students' scores for Part 1 to the building principal *no later than five calendar days prior to the date of the written test.* A sample reporting sheet is provided on page 15.

When students with disabilities take the Second Language Proficiency Examinations, you must provide them with the same specialized/adaptive equipment, instruction/demonstration techniques, and test accommodations specified in their Individualized Educational Program (IEP) or Section 504 Accommodation Plan (504 Plan). It is the responsibility of the principal to ensure that these accommodations are provided. In addition, when determining who should be tested, administrators must consider those students with disabilities who attend programs operated by the Board of Cooperative Educational Services (BOCES), as well as any other programs located outside the school.

Section 100.5(d) of the Commissioner's Regulations allows students who have acquired proficiency without completing a unit of study to earn one unit of credit by achieving a score of at least 85% on the examination and by meeting the requirements as stated in the Regulations. Since the speaking skills of such students cannot be evaluated in daily classroom activities (Part 1a), their score for the entire Part 1 will be based solely on their performance on the formal speaking test (Part 1b), which must be administered to them during the period from April 1 until five days prior to the date of the written test in June. To arrive at a total Part 1 score, prorate such students' score for Part 1b by multiplying it by 1.5. Since scores of Part 1 are to be expressed in whole numbers only, you may need to round up the score to the next whole number. *Example:* A student wishes to take a modern language proficiency examination without having completed a unit of study. If the student achieves a score of 15 on Part 1b, the formal speaking test, this student's total score for Part 1 is 23 (15 X 1.5 = 22.5 = 23).

PART 1a: INFORMAL CLASSROOM EVALUATION

Description

Scores for Part 1a of the examination are based on the students' performance in daily classroom activities during the designated assessment period. This assessment presumes that instruction routinely includes frequent opportunities for students to engage in a variety of realistic oral communications. These communications must be consistent with functions, topics, and situations for listening/speaking outcomes at Checkpoint A in the State syllabus. **Reading aloud and recitation of memorized text do not constitute oral communication for the purpose of this assessment.**

You must use the rubric provided on page 12 to assess student performance on Part 1a.

Using the Rubric

The rubric describes a continuum of performance from Level 4 (most proficient) to Level 1 (least proficient) on each of six criteria, called dimensions: initiation, response, conversational strategies, vocabulary, structure, and cultural appropriateness. Determine a student's raw score on each dimension by evaluating the student's classroom oral communication in terms of the characteristics for that dimension. The raw score represents the extent to which the student exhibits proficiency on that dimension. Add the student's raw scores for the six dimensions to determine a total raw score, which is then converted to the total number of credits for Part 1a, using the conversion chart below.

Part 1a Conversion Chart									
Total Raw Score	22–24	19–21	17–18	14–16	12–13	10–11	7–9	5–6	3–4	1–2
Total Credits	10	9	8	7	6	5	4	3	2	1

To facilitate scoring the student's Part 1a performance, use a score sheet in conjunction with the rubric. A sample score sheet is provided on page 13.

In applying the dimensions initiation and conversational strategies, keep in mind the following explanations and examples:

Dimension	Explanation	Examples
Initiation	Use of attention-getting devices to initiate a conversation	"Hello," "Excuse me," "Good morning"
Conversational Strategies	Ways to clarify and continue a conversation; students should use some or all of these strategies, as appropriate to the conversation.	*(see below)*
• Circumlocution	Use of familiar vocabulary and structures to express meaning beyond the student's current level of knowledge	Instead of saying "tiger," student says "a big cat with stripes in the zoo"
• Survival Skills	Use of learned expressions in appropriate situations to sustain conversation	"Please explain," "please repeat," "how do you say," "I don't understand"
	Use of nonverbal cues to clarify meaning	Facial expression, body language

• Intonation	Use of language-appropriate inflection to indicate purpose of utterance	Rising pitch to show question
• Self-Correction	Use of self-correction to clarify meaning	"You go ... no, I go"
• Response to Verbal Cues	Use of utterances of conversation partner as a clue or resource for unfamiliar vocabulary and structures for correcting, clarifying, or restating the student's own utterances	A—Give me a thing to write with. B—OK. Do you want a pen or a pencil? A—I need a pencil.

PART 1b: FORMAL SPEAKING TEST

Description

Part 1b of the examination, the formal speaking test, consists of communication tasks to be performed by students with their teacher. Each task prescribes a simulated conversation in which the student always plays the role of himself or herself, and you assume the specific role indicated in each task. Each student performs a total of four tasks, one in each of four categories consistent with the four communication functions specified in the State syllabus: (A) socializing, (B) providing/obtaining information, (C) expressing personal feelings, and (D) getting others to adopt a course of action (persuasion). Each task consists of a brief statement in English to indicate the purpose and setting of the communication, the person who is to initiate the conversation, and the role of the teacher. Each task is designed so that it can be completed in four interactions between the student and you. For the purpose of this manual, the student's part in each of these interactions is defined as an *utterance*.

Selection of the Part 1b Speaking Tasks

The State Education Department provides a collection of speaking tasks in the publication *Sourcebook of Speaking Tasks for Part 1*. The speaking tasks are grouped in categories by the four communication functions specified in the State syllabus: (A) socializing, (B) providing/obtaining information, (C) expressing personal feelings, and (D) getting others to adopt a course of action (persuasion). For each category, the sourcebook provides 86 to 88 tasks. Schools are to select 20 tasks per category, for a total of 80 speaking tasks that constitute Part 1b of a Second Language Proficiency Examination in a modern language. Since the sourcebook is not revised on an annual basis, it serves as the source of the Part 1b speaking test for current and future administrations of the examinations. **The sourcebook contains secure examination material and must be kept under lock and key when not in use.**

Select speaking tasks for Part 1b of the June examination as early in the school year as possible. For each successive June administration of the speaking test, a new set of 80 tasks must be selected, 20 tasks per category. Each succeeding set of 20 tasks must not have been used in the preceding administration of the speaking test. The selection of the speaking test tasks for the June examination in the current school year must be made before students have the opportunity to practice with the remainder of the speaking tasks in the sourcebook. The principal should take all necessary precautions to ensure that the Part 1b speaking test tasks to be administered in June of the current school year are kept secure.

The following procedures are recommended for the selection of the Part 1b speaking test:

- Select the 20 tasks per communication function category (total of 80 tasks) from the sourcebook, taking care not to select any tasks that were used on the most recent administration of the examination.
- Make a photocopy of each page of the sourcebook containing any of the 80 tasks.
- Remove the 80 speaking tasks from the photocopied pages and mount them on index cards, one task per card. Keep the index cards for the 20 tasks in each category in a separate group.
- At the test administration, the student picks one card from the category that you identify and hands the card to you. You read the task aloud to the student.

OR

- Select the 20 tasks per communication function category (total of 80 tasks) from the sourcebook, taking care not to select any tasks that were used on the most recent administration of the examination.
- Renumber the selected tasks from A1 to A20 (socializing); from B21 to B40 (providing/obtaining information); from C41 to C60 (expressing personal feelings); and from D61 to D80 (getting others to adopt a course of action [persuasion]). Also number small slips of paper from A1 through A20, B21 through B40, C41 through C60, and D61 through D80. Put the numbered slips in four boxes according to the four categories.
- At the test administration, the student picks a number from the box that you identify and hands the number to you. You locate the task that corresponds to the number and read the task aloud to the student.

For any given school year, you may use the tasks not selected for the June examination for instructional purposes. However, be careful to ensure that the complete set of printed speaking tasks in the sourcebook is kept secure at all times.

Administration and Rating

The formal speaking test is to be administered individually to each student, either in the presence of other students or with you alone, at the school's convenience from April 1 until five calendar days prior to the date of the written test. All four tasks need not be administered to each student at one sitting; they may be administered one task at a time over the entire speaking test period. **The Part 1b speaking tasks must be kept secure from the time they are initially selected at the beginning of the school year to the end of the speaking test period.**

Each student may perform only one task in each category. This task is to be selected at random from the tasks previously selected to constitute Part 1b. Depending on the administration method used by you or the school, the student will either:

- Pick an index card from the unnumbered cards in the category identified by you, hand it to you, and you will read the task aloud to the student.

OR

- Pick a numbered slip from the box identified by you and hand it to you. You will then locate the task in the sourcebook that corresponds to that number and will read the task aloud to the student.

Once the student has selected a task, it cannot be substituted for another or done over if the first performance is unsatisfactory.

In administering the test, you have two major responsibilities: (1) to rate the student's performance and (2) to act as the student's conversation partner.

As the rater, you can give a maximum of _five_ credits for each task according to the following criteria:

- One credit for each of the four student utterances that is comprehensible and appropriate. _Comprehensibility_ means that the utterance would make sense to native speakers who know no English but are used to foreigners trying to speak their language. *Appropriateness* means that the utterance contributes to the completion of the task.

- *Quality Credit:* One credit for the *quality* of all four comprehensible and appropriate student utterances. For each task, a student who requires three or more second attempts does not qualify for the quality credit. In addition, responses eligible for the quality credit must contain evidence from *each* of the following categories, as appropriate to Checkpoint A of the State syllabus:
  - Fluency may be demonstrated by, but is not limited to, ability to sustain the conversation, spontaneity, efficiency of task completion, intonation, pronunciation, and exclusive use of the target language.
  - Complexity may be demonstrated by, but is not limited to, ability to initiate and direct conversation, risk taking, creativity, choice and variety of vocabulary, and grammatical structures.
  - Accuracy may be demonstrated by, but is not limited to, correct grammatical structure, use of self-correction strategies, and cultural appropriateness.

As the conversation partner, you apply real-life communication devices in the target language to keep the student on task and to ensure the continuity of the conversation. Communication devices such as "Sorry, I didn't understand that," "Would you say that again, please," or "No, what I meant was ..." could be used in the target language for that purpose. An additional responsibility you have as the conversation partner is to bring the conversation to a natural conclusion.

As the conversation partner and rater, you may make two attempts at eliciting each of the four student utterances. If the student produces no comprehensible and appropriate utterance after your first two eliciting attempts at the very beginning of the conversation, the student receives no credit for the entire task. However, during the conversation, if a student produces no comprehensible and appropriate utterance after your second eliciting attempt, the student receives no credit for that utterance, and you shift to another aspect of the task.

To facilitate rating while acting as the conversation partner, the teacher should use a score sheet to keep track of the student's comprehensible and appropriate utterances, to record the number of eliciting attempts for each, and to determine whether the quality credit is warranted. A sample score sheet is provided on page 14. Certain teacher-student interactions, although natural in the course of a conversation, do not provide evidence of the student's ability to produce language. Disregard them for rating purposes. Examples of such interactions include:

- "yes-no" responses,
- restatements of all or essential parts of what you have said,
- proper names used in isolation, and
- socializing devices ("Hello," "How are you," etc.) except in socializing tasks where appropriate.

---

* At times, the task that the student selects may not be appropriate for that student, usually due to a student's particular disability or religious beliefs. In such cases, that student should be allowed to substitute another task. In order for the student with the disability to be eligible to substitute a task, that student must have been identified by the school district's Committee on Special Education as having a disability, and the need for the substitution must be consistent with the student's Individualized Education Program (IEP). A student is eligible to substitute tasks due to religious beliefs if it can be demonstrated that the student has been excused from participating in similar conversational situations during the school year.

Sample Administration of a Task

The student has randomly selected the following task:

> B31. [Student initiates] You say: You are in a store, looking at clothes. I am a salesclerk. You are going to tell me what you are looking for. You will start the conversation.

Presentation of the Task

Teacher Says	Student Says
English: You are in a store looking at clothes. I am a sales clerk. You are going to tell me what you are looking for. You will start the conversation. Do you understand the situation?	*English:* Yes, I think so.
English: All right. Remember that we are in a store, and you are looking at some clothes. I will give you a few seconds to think about what you may want to say in (target language) in this situation. (short pause)	
English: All right. Are you ready? From now on, we'll use no more English.	*English:* Yes, I think so.

Task Begins

Teacher Says	Student Says	Rating
(1)	(Target Language): Pardon me...	Student initiated conversation. Socializing device: disregard for rating purposes. Student has two more opportunities for first utterance. Teacher should make first eliciting attempt.
(Target Language): Hello. Can I help you find something?	(T.L.): I want ... (unintelligible sounds)	Incomprehensible. Student has one more opportunity for first utterance. Teacher should make second eliciting attempt.
(T.L.): Sorry, I did not understand. Please tell me what you want.	(T.L.): I want sweat air. (mispronunciation of word)	1 credit: Comprehensible and appropriate.
(2) (T.L.): Oh, you would like to see sweaters! — for anyone in particular?	(T.L.): For mine ...	Incomprehensible. Student has one more opportunity for this utterance. Teacher should make second eliciting attempt.
(T.L.): For whom did you say?	(T.L.): For mineself. (pointing to himself/herself)	1 credit: Comprehensible and appropriate.
(3) (T.L.): I see — for yourself. What color would you like?	(T.L.): I like cheap.	Comprehensible but inappropriate. Student has one more opportunity for this utterance. Teacher should make second eliciting attempt.
(T.L.): All these sweaters are inexpensive. Do you like dark colors or bright colors?	(T.L.): Bright.	Restatement. Disregard. Teacher should make second eliciting attempt again.
(T.L.): Which bright colors?	Shrugs shoulders, says nothing.	0 credit: No utterance.
(4) (T.L.): H m m ... I guess you don't know. How about this sweater?	(T.L.): Yes, I buy.	1 credit: Comprehensible and appropriate.

Task Ends

NOTE: This student will not receive the quality credit for the following reasons:

Although the student required less than three second attempts for the task, the student did not demonstrate evidence of fluency, completeness, and accuracy, as appropriate to Checkpoint A of the State syllabus.

In terms of fluency, the student's utterances did not demonstrate evidence of the ability to sustain the conversation and lacked spontaneity and efficiency of task completion. In terms of complexity, the student's utterances did not demonstrate evidence of the ability to initiate/direct conversation and showed little risk taking, creativity, or choice and variety of vocabulary and grammatical structures relevant to Checkpoint A. In terms of accuracy, the student's utterances did not demonstrate evidence of the ability to use correct grammatical structures or to use self-correction strategies consistent with Checkpoint A.

The following score sheet illustrates the rating of this task.

> You must write all scores for Part 1 of the Second Language Proficiency Examinations in modern languages **in ink** and submit completed score sheets to the principal's office no later than five calendar days before the date of the written test.

SECOND LANGUAGE PROFICIENCY EXAMINATIONS: MODERN LANGUAGES
Part 1b: Formal Speaking Test
Sample Score Sheet

Student's Name: _____Jason Talloway_____   Date: _____

	Utterance		First Attempt	Second Attempt	
Task: A _____ Task No.	1. 2. 3. 4.	(____) *	_____ _____ _____ _____ _____	_____ _____ _____ _____	Quality: _____ Total: _____
Task: B __31__ Task No.	1. 2. 3. 4.	(✓) *	0 0 0 1	1 1 0	Quality: 0 Total: 3
Task: C _____ Task No.	1. 2. 3. 4.	(____) *	_____ _____ _____ _____	_____ _____ _____ _____	Quality: _____ Total: _____
Task: D _____ Task No.	1. 2. 3. 4.	(____) *	_____ _____ _____ _____	_____ _____ _____ _____	Quality: _____ Total: _____

* Use a checkmark to indicate student's initiation of the conversation, if required.

SECOND LANGUAGE PROFICIENCY EXAMINATIONS: MODERN LANGUAGES
Part 1a: Informal Speaking Evaluation
Rubric

Dimension	Performance Levels			
	4	**3**	**2**	**1**
Initiation	Eagerly initiates speech, using appropriate attention-getting devices. Easily asks questions and speaks spontaneously.	Is willing to initiate speech, using appropriate attention-getting devices. Asks questions and speaks evenly.	Sometimes initiates speech, using attention-getting devices. Sometimes asks questions and speaks hesitantly.	Is reluctant to initiate speech and struggles to ask questions. Speech is halting.
Response	Almost always responds appropriately to questions/statements.	Frequently responds appropriately to questions/statements.	Sometimes responds appropriately to questions/statements.	Rarely responds appropriately to questions/statements.
Conversational Strategies	Clarifies and continues conversation, using all or some of the following strategies: • circumlocution • survival strategies • intonation • self-correction • verbal cues	Uses all or some strategies, but may need occasional prompting.	Uses some strategies and needs frequent prompting to further the conversation.	Uses few strategies. Relies heavily on conversation partner to sustain conversation. Rarely responds, even with frequent prompting.
Vocabulary	Incorporates a variety of old and new vocabulary. Uses idiomatic expressions appropriate to topic. Speaks clearly and imitates accurate pronunciation.	Uses a variety of old and limited new vocabulary. Attempts to use idiomatic expressions appropriate to topic. Speaks clearly and attempts accurate pronunciation.	Relies on basic vocabulary. Speech is comprehensible in spite of mispronunciations.	Uses limited vocabulary. Mispronunciations impede comprehensibility.
Structure	Makes few errors in the following areas: • verbs in utterances, when necessary, with appropriate subject/verb agreement • noun and adjective agreement • correct word order and article adjectives Errors do not hinder comprehensibility.	Makes several errors in structure that do not affect overall comprehensibility.	Makes several errors that may interfere with comprehensibility.	Makes utterances that are so brief that there is little evidence of structure, and comprehensibility is impeded.
Cultural Appropriateness	Almost always uses/interprets cultural manifestations when appropriate to the task (e.g., greeting, leave taking, gestures, proximity, etc.).	Frequently uses/interprets cultural manifestations when appropriate to the task.	Sometimes uses/interprets cultural manifestations when appropriate to the task.	Rarely uses/interprets cultural manifestations when appropriate to the task.

- A score of zero may be given for any of the dimensions if the student's performance falls below the criteria for Level 1.
- The student's total raw score is converted to the total number of credits for Part 1a using the conversion chart provided on page 4.

SECOND LANGUAGE PROFICIENCY EXAMINATIONS: MODERN LANGUAGES
Part 1a: Informal Speaking Evaluation
Sample Score Sheet

Student's Name: _____ **Date:** _____

Evaluate the student's classroom oral communication on each dimension according to the Part 1a rubric. For each dimension, determine the appropriate performance level (4, 3, 2, 1, or 0) and place a check mark in the appropriate column. Add these scores to determine the total raw score. Using the conversion chart below, convert the student's total raw score to the total number of credits for Part 1a.

Dimension	Performance Level				
	4	**3**	**2**	**1**	**0**
Initiation • Initiates speech and asks questions • Uses appropriate attention-getting devices • Speaks spontaneously					
Response • Responds appropriately to questions/statements					
Conversational Strategies • Circumlocution • Self-correction • Survival strategies • Verbal Cues • Intonation					
Vocabulary • Incorporates variety of old and new vocabulary • Uses idiomatic expressions appropriate to topic • Speaks clearly and imitates accurate pronunciation					
Structure • Uses verbs in utterances when necessary with appropriate subject/verb agreement • Makes nouns and adjectives agree • Uses correct word order and article adjectives					
Cultural Appropriateness • Uses/interprets cultural manifestations appropriate to the task (e.g., greeting, leave taking, gestures, proximity, etc.					

Total Raw Score _____

Total Number of Credits _____

Part 1a Conversion Chart									
Total Raw Score	22–24	19–21	17–18	14–16	12–13	10–11	7–9	5–6	3–4	1–2
Total Credits	10	9	8	7	6	5	4	3	2	1

SECOND LANGUAGE PROFICIENCY EXAMINATIONS: MODERN LANGUAGES
Part 1b: Formal Speaking Test
Sample Score Sheet

Student's Name: _____   Date: _____

	Utterance		First Attempt	Second Attempt	
Task: A _____ Task No.	1.	(___)	_____	_____	
	2.	*			
	3.		_____	_____	
	4.		_____	_____	Quality: _____
					Total: _____

	Utterance		First Attempt	Second Attempt	
Task: B _____ Task No.	1.	(___)	_____	_____	
	2.	*			
	3.		_____	_____	
	4.		_____	_____	Quality: _____
					Total: _____

	Utterance		First Attempt	Second Attempt	
Task: C _____ Task No.	1.	(___)	_____	_____	
	2.	*			
	3.		_____	_____	
	4.		_____	_____	Quality: _____
					Total: _____

	Utterance		First Attempt	Second Attempt	
Task: D _____ Task No.	1.	(___)	_____	_____	
	2.	*			
	3.		_____	_____	
	4.		_____	_____	Quality: _____
					Total: _____

* Use a checkmark to indicate student's initiation of the conversation, if required.

SECOND LANGUAGE PROFICIENCY EXAMINATIONS: MODERN LANGUAGES
Part 1: Speaking
Sample Reporting Sheet

(Complete in ink and submit to the principal's office at least five calendar days before the date of the written test.)

Student's Name	Part 1a*	Part 1b				
		Task				
		A +	B +	C +	D	= Part 1b*

* To be transferred to student's answer sheet for the written test.

Language _____ Class Period _____ Teacher _____

School _____ City or P.O. _____

Received in my office _____ _____
                              Date   *Principal's signature*

Useful Vocabulary

FRENCH USEFUL VOCABULARY: NOTE-WRITING

1.	Cher(s), Chère(s)	Dear
2.	M., Mme, Mlle	Mr., Mrs., Miss
3.	Je m'appelle…	My name is…
4.	Je voudrais…	I would like…
5.	Ça va?	How's it going?
6.	Comment vas-tu? Comment allez-vous?	How are you? (informal) How are you? (formal)
7.	Combien coûte _____?	How much does _____cost?
8.	Comment?	How? What?
9.	Qui?	Who?
10.	À quelle heure?	At what time?
11.	Quel/quelle? Quels/quelles?	Which?
12.	Pourquoi?	Why?
13.	parce que	because
14.	Aide-moi, s'il te plaît. Aidez-moi, s'il vous plaît.	Help me, please. (informal) Help me, please. (formal)
15.	Merci pour le cadeau/l'invitation. Merci pour ton aide. Merci pour votre aide.	Thanks for the gift/invitation. Thanks for your help. (informal) Thanks for your help. (formal)
16.	Bonne chance!	Good luck!
17.	Amuse-toi! Amusez-vous!	Have fun! (informal) Have fun! (formal)
18.	Écris-moi bientôt. Écrivez-moi bientôt.	Write soon. (informal) Write soon. (formal)
19.	Merci d'avance.	Thanks in advance.
20.	Mon numéro de téléphone est…	My phone number is…
21.	Mon adresse est…	My address is…

NOTE CLOSINGS

22.	Grosses bises,	Kisses, (very informal, familiar)
23.	Amitiés,	In friendship, (more formal)
24.	Sincèrement,	Sincerely, (formal)

FOR JOURNAL WRITING

25.	Mon journal:	My diary
26.	C'est aujourd'hui le _____. C'est aujourd'hui le deux juin.	Today is the _____ of _____. Today is the 2nd of June.

FRENCH USEFUL VOCABULARY: SOCIALIZING

1.	Comment t'appelles-tu? Comment vous appelez-vous?	What's your name? (informal) What's your name? (formal)
2.	Je m'appelle…	I call myself… (My name is…)
3.	Ça va? Comment vas-tu? Comment allez-vous?	How are you? (informal) How are you? (informal) How are you? (formal)
4.	Ça va bien, merci. Très bien, merci. Comme ci, comme ça. Ça ne va pas.	Fine, thanks. Very well, thanks. So, so. Not well.
5.	J'ai mal à la tête, à l'estomac, aux pieds.	My head hurts, my stomach hurts, my feet hurt.
6.	Quel âge as-tu? Quel âge avez-vous?	How old are you? (informal) How old are you? (formal)
7.	J'ai douze/treize ans.	I'm 12/13 years old.
8.	Comment es-tu? Comment êtes-vous?	What are you like? (informal) (Describe yourself) What are you like? (formal)
9.	Je suis grand(e), petit(e). Je suis intelligent(e). Je suis sportif/sportive. Je suis content(e), triste.	I am tall, short. I am intelligent, I am athletic. I am happy, sad.
10.	J'ai les cheveux bruns. J'ai les cheveux blonds. J'ai les cheveux noirs. J'ai les cheveux roux.	I have brown hair. I have blond hair. I have black hair. I have red hair.
11.	J'ai les yeux bleus. J'ai les yeux marron. J'ai les yeux verts.	I have blue eyes. I have brown eyes. I have green eyes.
12.	Où est-ce que tu habites? Où est-ce que vous habitez?	Where do you live? (informal) Where do you live? (formal)
13.	J'habite à New York.	I live in New York.

FRENCH USEFUL VOCABULARY: SOCIALIZING

14.	Tu es de quelle nationalité? Vous êtes de quelle nationalité?	What nationality are you? (informal) What nationality are you? (formal)
15.	Je suis américain(e). Je suis italien(ne). Je suis allemand(e). Je suis français(e). Je suis espagnol(e).	I am American. I am Italian. I am German. I am French. I am Spanish.
16.	Qu'est-ce que tu aimes faire?	What do you like to do?
17.	J'aime… -la musique rock -la cuisine chinoise, italienne, américaine, française -les devoirs -les sports -le cinéma	I like... -rock music -Chinese, Italian, American, French food -homework -sports -the movies
18.	J'aime... Je n'aime pas... -écouter la musique -regarder la télévision -danser -chanter	I like... I don't like... -to listen to music -to watch television -to dance -to sing

FRENCH USEFUL VOCABULARY: EXPRESSING FEELINGS

1.	J'aime... J'aime la pizza. J'aime la glace. J'aime les jeux vidéo. J'aime danser.	I like... I like pizza. I like ice cream. I like video games. I like to dance.
2.	Je n'aime pas...	I don't like...
3.	Je préfère, je veux, je désire	I prefer, I want, I desire
4.	Je ne préfère pas, je ne veux pas, je ne désire pas	I don't prefer, I don't want, I don't desire
5.	Je déteste...	I hate..., I dislike...
6.	*Les préférences:* -les jeux vidéo, les desserts, la pizza, la glace, le football américain, le musée, nager, danser, parler au téléphone	*Preferences:* -video games, desserts, pizza, ice cream, football, the museum, to swim, to dance, to talk on the phone
7.	Je suis triste, content(e).	I am sad, happy.
8.	Je suis sympa, timide, sincère, optimiste.	I am nice, shy, sincere, optimistic.
9.	Je voudrais aller... -au concert. -au théâtre. -au restaurant.	I would like to go... -to the concert. -to the theater. -to the restaurant.
10.	Quel est ton passe-temps favori? Quel est votre passe-temps favori?	What is your favorite pastime? (informal) What is your favorite pastime? (formal)
11.	Oui/Non	Yes/No
12.	C'est super !	It's great !
13.	C'est une bonne idée!	It's a good idea!
14.	Ça va.	It's o.k.
15.	Ça ne va pas.	It's not o.k.
16.	Je suis d'accord.	I agree.
17.	Je ne suis pas d'accord.	I don't agree.
18.	Moi aussi.	Me too.

FRENCH USEFUL VOCABULARY:
PROVIDING AND OBTAINING INFORMATION

1.	J'ai besoin d'aide/d'argent/ de directions.	I need help/money/directions.
2.	Où est le cinéma/l'hôtel/la maison/la gare?	Where is the movie theater/the hotel/the house/the train station?
3.	Combien coûte le billet/le stylo/la chambre?	How much does the ticket/pen/ room cost?
4.	Combien coûtent les billets/les stylos/les chambres?	How much do the tickets/pens/ rooms cost?
5.	Il/elle coûte vingt euros.	It costs twenty euros.
6.	Ils/elles coûtent vingt euros.	They cost twenty euros.
7.	Qui arrive à l'aéroport?	Who is arriving at the airport?
8.	Mon ami(e) arrive à l'aéroport.	My friend is arriving at the airport.
9.	Comment vas-tu?	How are you? (informal)
	Comment allez-vous?	How are you? (formal)
10.	Je vais bien.	I'm fine.
11.	Comment est-il/elle?	What is he/she like?
12.	Il/elle est grand(e) et mince.	He/she is tall and thin.
13.	À quelle heure commence le film?	What time does the movie begin ?
14.	Il commence à six heures.	It begins at six o' clock.
15.	À quelle heure arrives-tu?	What time are you arriving? (informal)
	À quelle heure arrivez-vous?	What time are you arriving? (formal)
16.	J'arrive à midi.	I arrive at noon.
17.	Qu'est-ce que tu vas acheter?	What are you going to buy? (informal)
	Qu'est-ce que vous allez acheter?	What are you going to buy? (formal)
18.	Qu'est-ce tu vas faire après l'école?	What are you going to do after school? (informal)
	Qu'est-ce que vous allez faire après l'école?	What are you going to do after school? (formal)
19.	Qu'est-ce que tu vas faire samedi?	What are you going to do on Saturday ? (informal)
	Qu'est-ce que vous allez faire samedi?	What are you going to do on Saturday ? (formal)

FRENCH USEFUL VOCABULARY:
PROVIDING AND OBTAINING INFORMATION

20. Qu'est-ce que tu vas faire ce soir?	What are you going to do tonight? (informal)
Qu'est-ce que vous allez faire ce soir ?	What are you going to do tonight? (formal)
21. Qu'est-ce que tu vas commander au restaurant ?	What are you going to order in the restaurant? (informal)
Qu'est-ce que vous allez commander au restaurant ?	What are you going to order in the restaurant? (formal)
22. Pourquoi est-ce que tu ne vas pas à l'école?	Why aren't you going to school? (informal)
Pourquoi est-ce que vous n'allez pas à l'école?	Why aren't you going to school? (formal)
23. J'ai mal à la gorge.	I have a sore throat.
24. Je suis malade.	I'm sick.
25. Prends une aspirine.	Take an aspirin. (informal)
Prenez une aspirine.	Take an aspirin. (formal)
26. Va chez le docteur.	Go to the doctor. (informal)
Allez chez le docteur.	Go to the doctor. (formal)
27. Reste au lit.	Stay in bed. (informal)
Restez au lit.	Stay in bed. (formal)
28. Aide-moi, s'il te plaît.	Help me, please. (informal)
Aidez-moi, s'il vous plaît.	Help me, please. (formal)

FRENCH USEFUL VOCABULARY: PERSUADING

1. Viens avec moi, s'il te plaît. Venez avec moi, s'il vous plaît.	Come with me, please. (informal) (formal)
2. Je désire manger, faire du vélo, faire du sport, aller à la plage, rester chez moi.	I want to eat, ride a bike, play sports, go to the beach, stay home.

3. Il faut…
   -étudier.
   -visiter Paris.
   -faire les devoirs.
   -organiser les papiers.
   -mettre la table.
   -faire la vaisselle.
   -aller chez le docteur.
	It is necessary…
	   -to study.
	   -to visit Paris.
	   -to do homework.
	   -to organize papers.
	   -to set the table.
	   -to wash the dishes.
	   -to go to the doctor.

4. Il y a un problème.	There is a problem.
5. Je n'ai pas d'argent/de temps.	I don't have money/time.
6. C'est impossible.	It is impossible.
7. C'est horrible.	It is horrible.
8. C'est dommage.	It is a shame.
9. C'est trop cher.	It is too expensive.
10. C'est bon marché.	It is inexpensive.
11. C'est loin.	It is far.
12. C'est long.	It is long.

13. D'abord, allons…
   -à la piscine.
   -au parc.
   -au centre commercial.
	First, let's go…
	   -to the pool.
	   -to the park.
	   -to the mall.

14. Et après, allons…
   -au restaurant.
   -chez moi.
   -au cinéma.
	And after, let's go…
	   -to the restaurant.
	   -to my house.
	   -to the movies.

15. D'accord.	Ok.
16. C'est super.	It's great.
17. C'est intéressant.	It's interesting.
18. C'est beau.	It's beautiful.
19. C'est comique.	It's funny.
20. C'est une bonne idée.	It's a good idea.

GERMAN USEFUL VOCABULARY: NOTE-WRITING

1.	Lieber/Liebe/Liebes	Dear (m/f/n)
2.	Herr, Frau, Fräulein	Mr., Mrs., Miss
3.	Ich heiße….; mein Name ist …	My name is…
4.	Ich möchte…	I would like…
5.	Wie geht's?	How are things going?
6.	Wie geht es dir?	How are you? (informal)
	Wie geht es Ihnen?	How are you? (formal)
7.	Wieviel ist …. ?	How much is . . .?
8.	Wie?	How?
9.	Wer?	Who?
10.	Um wieviel Uhr?	At what time?
11.	Welcher?/Welche?/Welches?	Which? (m/f/n)
12.	Warum?	Why?
13.	denn	because
14.	Hilf mir, bitte!	Help me, please. (informal)
	Helfen Sie mir, bitte!	Help me, please. (formal)
15.	Danke für das Geschenk!	Thanks for the gift.
	Danke für die Einladung!	Thanks for the invitation.
	Danke für deine Hilfe!	Thanks for your help. (informal)
	Danke für Ihre Hilfe!	Thanks for your help. (formal)
16.	Viel Glück!	Good luck!
17.	Viel Spaß!	Have a good time!
18.	Schreib bald!	Write soon. (informal)
	Schreiben Sie bald!	Write soon. (formal)
19.	Danke im voraus.	Thanks in advance.
20.	Meine Telefonnummer ist ….	My phone number is…
21.	Meine Adresse ist ….	My address is…

NOTE CLOSINGS

22.	Mit lieben Grüßen!	With affection. (informal)
23.	Dein, Deine	Yours (m/f) (informal)
24.	Mit freundlichen Grüßen!	Sincerely, (more formal)

FOR JOURNAL WRITING

25.	Mein Tagebuch.	My diary
26.	Heute ist der ___ ____	Today is the ____ of ____.
	Heute ist der zweite Juni.	Today is the 2nd of June.

GERMAN USEFUL VOCABULARY: SOCIALIZING

1.	Wie heißt du?	What's your name? (informal)
	Wie heißen Sie?	What's your name? (formal)
2.	Ich heiße …	My name is...
3.	Wie geht's?	How are things going?
	Wie geht es dir?	How are you? (informal)
	Wie geht es Ihnen?	How are you? (formal)
4.	Es geht mir gut, danke.	Fine, thanks.
	Sehr gut.	Very well, thanks.
	Es geht.	So, so.
	Nicht so gut.	Not so well.
5.	Der Kopf tut mir weh.	My head hurts.
	Der Bauch und	My stomach and
	die Füße tun mir weh.	my feet hurt.
6.	Wie alt bist du?	How old are you? (informal)
	Wie alt sind Sie?	How old are you? (formal)
7.	Ich bin zwölf/dreizehn Jahre alt.	I'm 12/13 years old.
8.	Wie siehst du aus?	What do you look like? (informal)
	Wie sehen Sie aus?	(formal)
9.	Ich bin groß, klein.	I am tall, short.
	Ich bin intelligent.	I am intelligent,
	Ich bin sportlich.	I am athletic.
	Ich bin glücklich/traurig.	I am happy, sad.
10.	Ich habe braune Haare.	I have brown hair.
	Ich habe blonde Haare.	I have blond hair.
	Ich habe schwarze Haare.	I have black hair.
	Ich habe rote Haare.	I have red hair.
11.	Ich habe blaue Augen.	I have blue eyes.
	Ich habe braune Augen.	I have brown eyes.
	Ich habe dunkle Augen.	I have dark eyes.
12.	Wo wohnst du?	Where do you live? (informal)
	Wo wohnen Sie?	Where do you live? (formal)
13.	Ich wohne in New York.	I live in New York.

GERMAN USEFUL VOCABULARY: SOCIALIZING

14.	Woher kommst du?	Where are you from? (informal)
	Woher kommen Sie?	Where are you from? (formal)
15.	Ich bin Amerikaner/Amerikanerin.	I am American. (m/f)
	Ich bin Deutscher/Deutsche.	I am German. (m/f)
	Ich bin Franzose/Französin.	I am French. (m/f)
	Ich bin Italiener/Italienerin.	I am Italian. (m/f)
	Ich bin Spanier/Spanierin.	I am Spanish. (m/f)
16.	Was hast du gern?	What do you like? (informal)
	Was haben Sie gern?	What do you like? (formal)
17.	Ich habe Rockmusik gern.	I like rock music.
	Ich habe die deutsche Küche gern.	I like German food.
	Ich habe die französische Küche gern.	I like French food.
	Ich habe die chinesische Küche gern.	I like Chinese food.
	Ich habe die italienische Küche gern.	I like Italian food.
	Ich habe Hausaufgaben gern.	I like homework.
	Ich habe Sport gern.	I like sports.
	Ich sehe Filme gern.	I like to watch movies.
18.	Ich habe laute Musik nicht gern.	I don't like loud music.
	Ich sehe nicht gern fern.	I don't like to watch TV.
	Ich tanze nicht gern.	I don't like to dance.
	Ich singe nicht gern.	I don't like to sing.

GERMAN USEFUL VOCABULARY: EXPRESSING FEELINGS

1.	Ich habe Pizza gern.	I like pizza.
	Ich habe Eis gern.	I like ice cream.
	Ich habe Videospiele gern.	I like video games.
	Ich habe Tanzen gern.	I like to dance.
2.	Ich habe _____ nicht gern.	I don't like…
	Ich will nicht ...	I don't want…
3.	Ich habe _____ lieber.	I prefer ...
4.	Lieber nicht.	Preferably not.
5.	Ich hasse...	I hate...
6.	*Die Vorlieben:*	*Preferences:*
	- Videospiele, Nachtische, Pizza, Eis, amerikanische Football, Museen, Schwimmen, Tanzen, Telefonieren	-video games, desserts, pizza, ice cream, football, museums, swimming, dancing, talking on the phone
7.	Ich bin traurig, froh, nett.	I am sad, happy, nice.
8.	Ich bin scheu, offen, optimistisch.	I am shy, sincere, optimistic.
9.	Ich möchte gern ins Konzert gehen.	I would like to go to the concert.
	Ich möchte gern ins Theater gehen.	I would like to go to the theater.
	Ich möchte gern ins Restaurant gehen	I would like to go to the restaurant.
10.	Was machst du in der Freizeit am liebsten?	What do you like to do best in your free time? (informal)
	Was machen Sie in der Freizeit am liebsten?	What do you like to do best in your free time? (formal)
11.	Ja/Nein	Yes/No
12.	Das ist prima!	That's great!
13.	Das ist eine gute Idee!	That's a good idea!
14.	Das ist in Ordnung; das ist OK.	That's o.k.
15.	Das ist nicht in Ordnung; das ist nicht OK.	That's not o.k.
16.	Stimmt.	That's correct.
17.	Stimmt nicht.	That's not correct.
18.	Ich auch.	Me too.

GERMAN USEFUL VOCABULARY:
PROVIDING AND OBTAINING INFORMATION

1.	Ich brauche Hilfe, Geld, Informationen.	I need help/money/directions.
2.	Wo ist das Kino, das Hotel, das Haus, der Bahnhof?	Where is the movie theater/the hotel/the house/the train station?
3.	Wieviel kostet die Karte, der Bleistift, das Zimmer?	How much does the ticket/pencil/room cost?
4.	Wieviel kosten die Karten, die Bleistifte, die Zimmer?	How much do the tickets/pencils/rooms cost?
5.	Er/sie/es kostet zwanzig Euro.	It (m/f/n) costs twenty euros.
6.	Sie kosten zwanzig Euro.	They cost twenty euros.
7.	Wer kommt am Flughafen an?	Who is arriving at the airport?
8.	Mein Freund/Meine Freundin kommt am Flughafen an.	My friend (m/f) is arriving at the airport.
9.	Wie geht es dir? Wie geht es Ihnen?	How are you? (informal) How are you? (formal)
10.	Es geht mir gut.	I'm fine.
11.	Wie sieht er/sie aus?	What does he/she look like?
12.	Er/sie ist groß und schlank.	He/she is tall and thin.
13.	Um wieviel Uhr beginnt der Film?	What time does the movie begin ?
14.	Er beginnt um sechs Uhr.	It begins at six o' clock.
15.	Um wieviel Uhr kommst du an? Um wieviel Uhr kommen Sie an?	What time are you arriving? (informal) What time are you arriving? (formal)
16.	Ich komme zu Mittag an.	I'll arrive at noon.
17.	Was kaufst du? Was kaufen Sie?	What are you going to buy? (informal) What are you going to buy? (formal)
18.	Was machst du nach der Schule? Was machen Sie nach der Schule?	What are you going to do after school? (informal) What are you going to do after school? (formal)
19.	Was machst du am Samstag? Was machen Sie am Samstag?	What are you going to do on Saturday ? (informal) What are you going to do on Saturday ? (formal)

GERMAN USEFUL VOCABULARY:
PROVIDING AND OBTAINING INFORMATION

20. Was machst du heute abend?	What are you going to do tonight? (informal)
Was machen Sie heute abend?	What are you going to do tonight? (formal)
21. Was bestellst du im Restaurant?	What are you going to order in the restaurant? (informal)
Was bestellen Sie im Restaurant?	What are you going to order in the restaurant? (formal)
22. Warum gehst du nicht zur Schule?	Why aren't you going to school? (informal)
Warum gehen Sie nicht zur Schule?	Why aren't you going to school? (formal)
23. Ich habe Halsschmerzen.	I have a sore throat.
24. Ich bin krank.	I'm sick.
25. Nimm Aspirin!	Take an aspirin. (informal)
Nehmen Sie Aspirin!	Take an aspirin. (formal)
26. Geh zum Arzt!	Go to the doctor. (informal)
Gehen Sie zum Arzt!	Go to the doctor. (formal)
27. Bleib im Bett!	Stay in bed. (informal)
Bleiben Sie im Bett!	Stay in bed. (formal)
28. Hilf mir, bitte!	Help me, please. (informal)
Helfen Sie mir, bitte!	Help me, please. (formal)

GERMAN USEFUL VOCABULARY: PERSUADING

1.	Komm bitte mit! Kommen Sie bitte mit!	Come with me, please. (informal) (formal)
2.	Ich möchte essen, radfahren, Sport treiben, zum Strand gehen, zu Hause bleiben.	I want to eat, ride a bike, play sports, go to the beach, stay home.

3.	Man muß…
	  -lernen.
	  -Deutschland besuchen.
	  -Hausaufgaben machen.
	  -die Papiere organisieren.
	  -den Tisch decken.
	  -das Geschirr spülen.
	  -zum Arzt gehen.
		One must…
		  -study.
		  -visit Germany.
		  -do homework.
		  -organize papers.
		  -set the table.
		  -wash the dishes.
		  -go to the doctor.

4.	Es gibt ein Problem.	There is a problem.
5.	Ich habe kein Geld/keine Zeit.	I don't have money/time.
6.	Das ist nicht möglich.	It is impossible.
7.	Das ist schrecklich.	It is horrible.
8.	Das ist schade.	It's too bad.
9.	Das ist zu teuer.	It is too expensive.
10.	Das ist billig.	It is inexpensive.
11.	Das ist zu weit entfernt.	It is too far away.
12.	Das ist zu lang.	It is too long.

13.	Zuerst gehen wir...
	  -zum Schwimmbad!
	  -zum Park!
	  -ins Kino!
		First, let's go…
		  -to the pool.
		  -to the park.
		  -to the movies.

14.	Nachher gehen wir…
	  -ins Restaurant!
	  -zu mir!
	  -ins Kino!
		Then, let's go…
		  -to the restaurant.
		  -to my house.
		  -to the movies.

15.	Das ist in Ordnung. Das ist OK.	It's okay.
16.	Das ist toll, wunderbar.	It's great, wonderful.
17.	Das ist interessant.	It's interesting.
18.	Das ist schön.	It's beautiful/nice/fine.
19.	Das ist lustig.	It's amusing.
20.	Das ist eine gute Idee!	It's a good idea.

ITALIAN USEFUL VOCABULARY: NOTE-WRITING

1.	Caro/a	Dear
2.	Sig., Sig.ra, Sig.na	Mr., Mrs., Miss
3.	Mi chiamo…, Il mio nome è…	My name is…
4.	Io vorrei…/Mi piacerebbe…	I would like…
5.	Come va?	How are things going?
6.	Come stai?	How are you? (informal)
	Come sta?	How are you? (formal)
7.	Quanto/a, Quanti/e?	How much? How many?
8.	Come?	How?
9.	Chi?	Who?
10.	A che ora?	At what time?
11.	Quale? Quali?	Which?
12.	Perché?	Why?
13.	Perché	because
14.	Per favore, aiutami.	Please, help me. (informal)
	Per favore, mi aiuti.	Please, help me. (formal)
15.	Grazie per il regalo/l'invito.	Thanks for the gift/invitation.
	Grazie per il tuo aiuto.	Thanks for your help. (informal)
	Grazie per il Suo aiuto.	Thanks for your help. (formal)
16.	Buona fortuna!	Good luck!
17.	Divertiti!	Have fun! (informal)
	Si diverta!	Have fun! (formal)
18.	Scrivimi al più presto.	Write soon. (informal)
	Mi scriva al più presto.	Write soon. (formal)
19.	Grazie in anticipo.	Thanks in advance.
20.	Il mio numero di telefono è ...	My phone number is…
21.	Il mio indirizzo è ...	My address is…

NOTE CLOSINGS

22.	Con affetto,	With affection,
23.	Il tuo amico/ la tua amica,	Your friend,
24.	Distinti saluti,	Sincerely, Best regards,

FOR JOURNAL WRITING

25.	Caro diario,	Dear diary,
26.	Oggi è il _____	Today is the _____.
	Oggi è il due giugno.	Today is the 2nd of June.

ITALIAN USEFUL VOCABULARY: SOCIALIZING

1.	Come ti chiami?	What's your name? (informal)
	Come si chiama?	What's your name? (formal)
2.	Mi chiamo…	I call myself… (My name is...)
3.	Come va?	How are things going? (informal)
	Come stai?, Come ti senti?	How are you? (informal)
	Come sta?, Come si sente?	How are you? (formal)
4.	Bene grazie.	Fine, thanks.
	Molto bene, grazie.	Very well, thanks.
	Così, così.	So, so.
	Molto male.	Not well.
5.	Ho mal di testa, di stomaco	I have a headache, stomach
	e mi fanno male i piedi.	ache and my feet hurt.
6.	Quanti anni hai?	How old are you? (informal)
	Quanti anni ha?	How old are you? (formal)
7.	Ho dodici/tredici anni.	I'm 12/13 years old.
8.	Come sei?	What are you like? (informal)
		(Describe yourself)
	Com'è?	What are you like? (formal)
9.	Sono alto/a, basso/a.	I am tall, short.
	Sono intelligente.	I am intelligent,
	Sono atletico/a.	I am athletic.
	Sono felice, triste.	I am happy, sad.
10.	Ho i capelli castani.	I am a brunette.
	Ho i capelli biondi.	I am a blonde.
	Ho i capelli neri.	I have black hair.
	Ho i capelli rossi.	I am a redhead.
11.	Ho gli occhi blu.	I have blue eyes.
	Ho gli occhi castani.	I have brown eyes.
	Ho gli occhi scuri.	I have dark eyes.
12.	Dove abiti?	Where do you live? (informal)
	Dove abita?	Where do you live? (formal)
13.	Abito a New York.	I live in New York.

ITALIAN USEFUL VOCABULARY: SOCIALIZING

14.	Di che nazionalità sei? Di che nazionalità è?	What nationality are you? (informal) What nationality are you? (formal)
15.	Sono americano/a. Sono italiano/a. Sono tedesco/a. Sono francese. Sono spagnolo/a.	I am American. I am Italian. I am German. I am French. I am Spanish.
16.	Che cosa ti piace fare?	What do you like to do?
17.	Mi piace… (singular) -la musica rock -la cucina cinese, italiana, americana, francese Mi piacciono… (plural) - i compiti - gli sport - i film	I like... -rock music -Chinese, Italian, American, French food I like... -homework -sports -the movies
18.	Mi piace/io amo… Non mi piace…, non amo… -ascoltare la musica -guardare la televisione. -ballare -cantare	I like/ I love… I don't like/I don't love… -to listen to music -to watch television -to dance -to sing

ITALIAN USEFUL VOCABULARY: EXPRESSING FEELINGS

1.	Mi piace (piacciono)/io amo… Mi piace la pizza. Mi piace il gelato. Mi piacciono i videogiochi. Mi piace ballare.	I like/ I love… I like pizza. I like ice cream. I like video games. I like to dance.
2.	Non mi piace (piacciono)/ non amo...	I don't like/ I don't love...
3.	Preferisco, voglio, desidero	I prefer, I want, I desire
4.	Non preferisco, non voglio, Non desidero	I don't prefer, I don't want, I don't desire
5.	Odio…, detesto…	I hate..., I dislike...
6.	*Preferenze:* - i videogiochi, i dolci, la pizza, il gelato, il calcio, il museo, nuotare, ballare, parlare al telefono	*Preferences:* -video games, desserts, pizza, ice cream, soccer, the museum, to swim, to dance, to talk on the phone
7.	Sono triste, contento/a, felice, allegro/a.	I am sad, happy.
8.	Sono simpatico/a, timido/a, sincero/a, ottimista.	I am nice, shy, sincere, optimistic.
9.	Vorrei andare… - al concerto. - al teatro. - al ristorante.	I would like to go -to the concert -to the theater -to the restaurant
10.	Qual è il tuo passatempo preferito? Qual è il Suo passatempo preferito?	What is your favorite pastime? (informal) What is your favorite pastime? (formal)
11.	Sì/No	Yes/No
12.	È fantastico!	It's great !
13.	È una buona idea!	It's a good idea!
14.	Va bene.	It's o.k.
15.	Non va bene.	It's not o.k.
16.	Sono d'accordo.	I agree.
17.	Non sono d'accordo.	I don't agree.
18.	Anche io.	Me too.

ITALIAN USEFUL VOCABULARY:
PROVIDING AND OBTAINING INFORMATION

1. Ho bisogno d'aiuto/di soldi/ di un indicazione stradale.	I need help/money/directions.
2. Dov'è il cinema/ l'albergo/ la casa/la stazione?	Where is the movie theater/the hotel/the house/the train station?
3. Quanto costa il biglietto/ la penna/la camera?	How much does the ticket/ pen/room cost?
4. Quanto costano i biglietti/ le penne/le camere?	How much do the tickets/ pens/rooms cost?
5. Costa venti euro.	It costs twenty euros.
6. Costano venti euro.	They cost twenty euros.
7. Chi arriva all'aeroporto?	Who is arriving at the airport?
8. Il mio amico/la mia amica arriva all'aeroporto.	My friend (m/f) is arriving at the airport.
9. Come stai? Come va?	How are you? (informal)
10. Sto bene.	I'm fine.
11. Lui / lei com'è?	What is he/she like?
12. Lui / lei è alto/a e magro/a.	He/she is tall and thin.
13. A che ora comincia il film? A che ora inizia il film?	What time does the movie begin ?
14. Comincia alle sei. Inizia alle sei.	It begins at six o' clock.
15. A che ora arrivi? \ \ A che ora arriva?	What time are you arriving? (informal) \ (formal)
16. Arrivo a mezzogiorno.	I'll arrive at noon.
17. Che cosa compri? \ \ Che cosa compra?	What are you going to buy? (informal) \ (formal)
18. Che cosa fai dopo scuola? \ \ Che cosa fa dopo scuola?	What are you going to do after school? (informal) \ What are you going to do after school? (formal)
19. Che cosa fai sabato? \ \ Che cosa fa sabato?	What are you going to do on Saturday ? (informal) \ What are you going to do on Saturday ? (formal)

20. Che cosa fai stasera?	What are you going to do tonight ? (informal)
Che cosa fa stasera?	What are you going to do tonight ? (formal)
21. Che cosa ordini al ristorante?	What are you going to order in the restaurant? (informal)
Che cosa ordina al ristorante?	What are you going to order in the restaurant? (formal)
22. Perché non vai a scuola?	Why aren't you going to school? (informal)
Perché non va a scuola?	Why aren't you going to school? (formal)
23. Ho mal di gola.	I have a sore throat.
24. Sto male / sono malato	I'm sick.
25. Prendi una aspirina. Prenda una aspirina.	Take an aspirin. (informal) Take an aspirin. (formal)
26. Va dal dottore (medico). Vada dal dottore (medico).	Go to the doctor. (informal) Go to the doctor. (formal)
27. Resta a letto. Resti a letto.	Stay in bed. (informal) Stay in bed. (formal)
28. Aiutami, per favore? Mi aiuti, per favore?	Help me, please. (informal) Help me, please. (formal)

ITALIAN USEFUL VOCABULARY: PERSUADING

1. Vieni con me, per favore. Venga con me, per favore.	Come with me, please. (informal) (formal)
2. Voglio mangiare, andare in bicicletta, fare sport, andare alla spiaggia, restare a casa.	I want to eat, ride a bike, play sports, go to the beach, stay home.
3. È necessario… -studiare. -visitare l'Italia. -fare i compiti. -organizzare le carte. -mettere la tavola. -lavare i piatti. -andare dal medico.	It is necessary… -to study. -to visit Italy. -to do homework. -to organize papers. -to set the table. -to wash the dishes. -to go to the doctor.
4. C'è un problema.	There is a problem.
5. Non ho soldi/tempo.	I don't have money/time.
6. È impossibile.	It is impossible.
7. È orribile.	It is horrible.
8. È un peccato (che peccato).	It is a shame.
9. È molto caro.	It is too expensive.
10. Non è molto caro.	It is inexpensive.
11. È molto lontano.	It is very far.
12. È lungo.	It is long.
13. Prima, andiamo... -alla piscina. -al parco. -al centro commerciale.	First, let's go… -to the pool. -to the park. -to the mall.
14. Dopo, andiamo… -al ristorante. -a casa mia. -al cinema.	Then we can go… -to the restaurant. -to my house. -to the movies.
15. Va bene.	It's ok.
16. È fantastico.	It's great.
17. È interessante.	It's interesting.
18. È bello/a.	It's pretty.
19. È comico.	It's funny.
20. È una buona idea.	It's a good idea.

SPANISH USEFUL VOCABULARY: NOTE-WRITING

1.	Querido/a, Queridos/as	Dear
2.	Sr., Sra., Srta.	Mr., Mrs., Miss
3.	Me llamo…, Mi nombre es…	My name is…
4.	Yo quisiera…/ Me gustaría…	I would like…
5.	¿Qué tal? ¿Qué pasa?	How are things going?
6.	¿Cómo estás?	How are you? (informal)
	¿Cómo está?	How are you? (formal)
7.	¿Cuánto es?	How much is?
8.	¿Cómo?	How?
9.	¿Quién?/¿Quiénes?	Who?
10.	¿A qué hora?	At what time?
11.	¿Cuál? ¿Cuáles?	Which?
12.	¿Por qué?	Why?
13.	porque	because
14.	Ayúdame, por favor.	Please, help me. (informal)
	Ayúdeme, por favor.	Please, help me. (formal)
15.	Gracias por el regalo, la invitación.	Thanks for the gift/invitation.
	Gracias por tu ayuda.	Thanks for your help. (informal)
	Gracias por su ayuda.	Thanks for your help. (formal)
16.	¡Buena suerte!	Good luck!
17.	¡Diviértete!	Have fun! (informal)
	¡Diviértase!	Have fun! (formal)
18.	Escríbeme pronto.	Write soon. (informal)
	Escríbame pronto.	Write soon. (formal)
19.	Gracias en avance.	Thanks in advance.
20.	Mi número de teléfono es…	My phone number is…
21.	Mi dirección es…	My address is…

NOTE CLOSINGS

22.	Con cariño,	With affection,
23.	Tu amigo/amiga,	Your friend,
24.	Atentamente,/Sinceramente,	Sincerely,

FOR JOURNAL WRITING

25.	Mi diario	My diary,
26.	Hoy es el ___ de ___.	Today is the _____ of ____.
	Hoy es el dos de junio.	Today is the 2nd of June.

SPANISH USEFUL VOCABULARY: SOCIALIZING

1.	¿Cómo te llamas?	What's your name? (informal)
	¿Cómo se llama?	What's your name? (formal)
2.	Me llamo…	I call myself… (My name is...)
3.	¿Cómo va? ¿Qué tal?	How are you? How are things going?
	¿Cómo estás?	How are you? (informal)
	¿Cómo está?	How are you? (formal)
4.	Bien, gracias.	Fine, thanks.
	Muy bien, gracias.	Very well, thanks.
	Así, así.	So, so.
	Muy mal.	Not well.
5.	Me duele la cabeza, el estómago, y me duelen los pies.	I have a headache, stomach ache and my feet hurt.
6.	¿Cuántos años tienes?	How old are you? (informal)
	¿Cuántos años tiene?	How old are you? (formal)
7.	Tengo doce/trece años.	I'm 12/13 years old.
8.	¿Cómo eres tú?	What are you like? (informal) (Describe yourself)
	¿Cómo es Ud.?	What are you like? (formal)
9.	Soy alto/a, bajo/a.	I am tall, short.
	Soy inteligente.	I am intelligent,
	Soy atlético/a.	I am athletic.
	Soy feliz, triste.	I am happy, sad.
10.	Tengo pelo castaño.	I am a brunette.
	Tengo pelo rubio.	I am a blonde.
	Tengo pelo negro.	I have black hair.
	Soy pelirrojo/a.	I am a redhead.
11.	Tengo los ojos azules.	I have blue eyes.
	Tengo los ojos pardos. (marrones)	I have brown eyes.
	Tengo los ojos oscuros.	I have dark eyes.
12.	¿Dónde vives?	Where do you live? (informal)
	¿Dónde vive?	Where do you live? (formal)
13.	Vivo en Nueva York.	I live in New York.

SPANISH USEFUL VOCABULARY: SOCIALIZING

14.	¿Cuál es tu nacionalidad?	What nationality are you? (informal)
	¿Cuál es su nacionalidad?	What nationality are you? (formal)
15.	Soy norteamericano/a.	I am American.
	Soy estadounidense.	I am from the U.S.
	Soy italiano/a.	I am Italian.
	Soy alemán/a.	I am German.
	Soy francés/a.	I am French.
	Soy dominicano/a.	I am Dominican.
	Soy mexicano/a.	I am Mexican.
	Soy español/a.	I am Spanish.
16.	¿Qué te gusta hacer?	What do you like to do?
17.	Me gusta… (singular)	I like...
	-la música rock	-rock music
	-la comida china, italiana americana y francesa.	-Chinese, Italian, American and French food
	-la tarea.	-homework.
	Me gustan… (plural)	I like...
	-los deportes.	-sports
	-las películas.	-the movies
18.	Me gusta…/me encanta…	I like.../I love...
	No me gusta…/no me encanta…	I don't like.../I don't love...
	-escuchar música	-to listen to music
	-mirar la televisión	-to watch television
	-bailar	-to dance
	-cantar	-to sing

SPANISH USEFUL VOCABULARY: EXPRESSING FEELINGS

1.	Me gusta(n)/me encanta(n)…	I like/I love…
	Me gusta la pizza.	I like pizza.
	Me gusta el helado.	I like ice cream.
	Me gustan los videojuegos.	I like video games.
	Me gusta bailar.	I like to dance.
2.	No me gusta(n)…	I don't like…
	No me encanta(n)…	I don't love…
3.	Prefiero, quiero, deseo	I prefer, I want, I desire
4.	No prefiero, no quiero,	I don't prefer, I don't want,
	No deseo	I don't desire
5.	Odio…, detesto…	I hate…, I dislike…
6.	*Las preferencias:*	*Preferences:*
	los videojuegos, los postres, la	video games, desserts, pizza,
	pizza el helado, el fútbol	ice cream, football, the
	americano, el museo, nadar,	museum, to swim,
	bailar, hablar por teléfono	to dance, to talk on the phone
7.	Estoy triste,	I am sad,
	contento/a, feliz, alegre.	happy.
8.	Soy simpático/a, tímido/a,	I am nice, shy,
	sincero/a, optimista.	sincere, optimistic.
9.	Quisiera ir…	I would like to go to…
	-al concierto	-the concert
	-al teatro	-the theater
	-al restaurante.	-the restaurant.
10.	¿Cuál es tu pasatiempo favorito?	What is your favorite pastime? (informal)
	¿Cuál es su pasatiempo favorito?	What is your favorite pastime? (formal)
11.	Sí/No	Yes/No
12.	¡Es fantástico!	It's great! It's fantastic!
13.	¡Es una buena idea!	It's a good idea!
14.	Está bien.	It's ok.
15.	No está bien.	It's not ok.
16.	Estoy de acuerdo.	I agree.
17.	No estoy de acuerdo.	I don't agree.
18.	Yo también.	Me too.

SPANISH USEFUL VOCABULARY:
PROVIDING AND OBTAINING INFORMATION

1.	Necesito ayuda, dinero, instrucciones.	I need help/money/directions.
2.	¿Dónde está el cine/el hotel/ la casa/ la estación del tren?	Where is the movie theater/the hotel/the house/the train station?
3.	¿Cuánto cuesta el boleto/ el bolígrafo/el cuarto?	How much does the ticket/pen/ room cost?
4.	¿Cuánto cuestan los boletos/ los bolígrafos/cuartos?	How much do the tickets/pens/ rooms cost?
5.	Cuesta veinte euros.	It costs twenty euros.
6.	Cuestan veinte euros.	They cost twenty euros.
7.	¿Quién llega al aeropuerto?	Who is arriving at the airport?
8.	Mi amigo/a llega al aeropuerto.	My friend (m/f) is arriving at the airport.
9.	¿Cómo estás? ¿Qué tal?	How are you? (informal)
10.	Estoy bien.	I'm fine.
11.	¿Cómo es ella/él?	What is he/she like?
12.	Es alto/a y flaco/a.	He/she is tall and thin.
13.	¿A qué hora empieza la película? ¿A qué hora comienza la película?	What time does the movie begin ?
14.	Empieza a las seis. Comienza a las seis.	It begins at six o' clock.
15.	¿A qué hora llegas tú? ¿A qué hora llega Ud.?	What time are you arriving? (informal) (formal)
16.	Llego al mediodía.	I arrive at noon.
17.	¿Qué vas a comprar? ¿Qué va a comprar?	What are you going to buy? (informal) (formal)
18.	¿Qué vas a hacer después de las clases? ¿Qué va a hacer después de las clases?	What are you going to do after school? (informal) What are you going to do after school? (formal)
19.	¿ Qué vas a hacer el sábado? ¿Qué va a hacer el sábado?	What are you going to do on Saturday ? (informal) What are you going to do on Saturday ? (formal)

SPANISH USEFUL VOCABULARY:
PROVIDING AND OBTAINING INFORMATION

20.	¿Qué vas a hacer esta noche?	What are you going to do tonight ? (informal)
	¿Qué va a hacer esta noche?	What are you going to do tonight ? (formal)
21.	¿Qué vas a pedir en el restaurante?	What are you going to order in the restaurant? (informal)
	¿Qué va a pedir en el restaurante?	What are you going to order in the restaurant? (formal)
22.	¿Por qué no vas a la escuela?	Why aren't you going to school? (informal)
	¿Por qué no va a la escuela?	Why aren't you going to school? (formal)
23.	Tengo dolor de garganta.	I have a sore throat.
24.	Estoy enfermo/a.	I'm sick.
25.	Toma una aspirina.	Take an aspirin. (informal)
	Tome una aspirina.	Take an aspirin. (formal)
26.	Ve al médico.	Go to the doctor. (informal)
	Vaya al médico.	Go to the doctor. (formal)
27.	Quédate en cama.	Stay in bed. (informal)
	Quédese en cama.	Stay in bed. (formal)
28.	Ayúdame, por favor.	Help me, please. (informal)
	Ayúdeme, por favor.	Help me, please. (formal)

SPANISH USEFUL VOCABULARY: PERSUADING

1. Ven conmigo, por favor. Venga conmigo, por favor.	Come with me, please. (informal) (formal)
2. Quiero comer, montar en bicicleta, jugar a los deportes, ir a la playa, quedarme en casa.	I want to eat, ride a bike, play sports, go to the beach, stay home.
3. Es necesario... -estudiar. -visitar España. -hacer la tarea. -organizar los papeles. -poner la mesa. -lavar los platos. -ir al médico.	It is necessary... -to study. -to visit Spain. -to do homework. -to organize papers. -to set the table. -to wash the dishes. -to go to the doctor.
4. Hay un problema.	There is a problem.
5. No tengo dinero/tiempo.	I don't have money/time.
6. Es imposible.	It is impossible.
7. Es horrible.	It is horrible.
8. Es lástima.	It is a shame.
9. Es muy caro/a.	It is very expensive.
10. Es barato/a.	It is inexpensive.
11. Está muy lejos.	It is very far.
12. Es largo.	It is long.
13. Primero, vamos... -a la piscina. -al parque. -al centro comercial.	First, let's go... -to the pool. -to the park. -to the mall.
14. Después, vamos... -al restaurante. -a mi casa. -al cine.	And after, let's go... -to the restaurant. -to my house. -to the movies.
15. Está bien.	It's ok.
16. Es fantástico.	It's great.
17. Es interesante.	It's interesting.
18. Es bonito/a.	It's beautiful.
19. Es cómico/a.	It's funny.
20. Es una buena idea.	It's a good idea.

Helpful Hints for Student Success on the N.Y.S. Proficiency Exam

The Proficiency Exam Writing Section
Helpful Hints for Students

1) Carefully read the Task Question. Be sure to accomplish the purpose of the writing question, as it is stated in the directions. **NO CREDIT** will be given unless the purpose of the writing task is accomplished.

2) Form a clear idea of to whom you are writing and decide if the task requires the use of the familiar or polite form of **YOU**. Maintain this form throughout your answer.

3) Jot down any useful sentences, expressions or words **before** writing in paragraph form.

4) On your test paper, at the end of each Writing Task Question, there is a series of useful suggestions listed to assist you. It is not necessary to use <u>all</u> of the listed suggestions as long as you accomplish the writing task's purpose and that you have written at least 30 words. You may add your own ideas, provided that they are in keeping with the task's purpose.

5) Organize and outline your ideas before you begin to write in paragraph form. Make sure your writing stays on the topic.

6) If you do not know a word, say something else. Do **NOT** write in English. Stick to the vocabulary expressions you learned in class and that you know very well. Try to use a variety of words.

7) The task requirement is a minimum of 30 words. Do your best to write more than 30 words. Partial credit will be given for fewer than 30 words.

8) Proofread your writing before handing in your exam. Check for:
   - ◆ spelling
   - ◆ grammar (adjective-noun agreement, subject-verb matching)
   - ◆ word count: a minimum of 30 words
   - ◆ Make sure your ideas fit together logically.

9) As you study during the year, maintain your own list of useful expressions and words. Frequently review this list and your class notes.

10) Practice will increase your opportunity for success.

Student Work Sheet: Note-Writing

Name: _____ Date: _____ Task #: _____

Brainstorming:
♦ Jot down useful words and expressions for your note:

_____   _____

_____   _____

_____   _____

Note-Writing:

_____:
(Salutation)

(Body of note:)

_____

_____

_____

_____

_____

                                        _____
                                                              (Closing)

Self-Evaluation:
    A) Word Count: _____
       Note: 1. Numbers, <u>unless written out</u>, do not count.
             2. Names of people do not count.
             3. Product names in English do not count.

    B) I have checked:
       _____ my spelling.
       _____ that my subjects and verbs match.
       _____ that my adjectives and nouns agree.
       _____ that I have fulfilled the purpose of the note.
       _____ that my ideas fit together logically.

    C) What I would like to learn/review for writing this note:

_____

_____

Student Writing Tasks

Personal Identification Writing Tasks

In the spaces provided, complete the following writing task. This writing task should be written entirely in the **target language** and should contain a minimum of **30 words**. First names of people **do not count**. Be sure that you satisfy the purpose of the task. The structure or expressions used should be connected logically and should demonstrate a wide range of vocabulary.

Topic A: You have just been given the name of your new pen pal. Write him/her a short note to introduce yourself in the *target language*. You may wish to include:

- ◆ Your name and age
- ◆ Your interests
- ◆ Your personality and physical qualities
- ◆ Questions you would like to ask him/her

Personal Identification Writing Tasks

In the spaces provided, complete the following writing task. This writing task should be written entirely in the **target language** and should contain a minimum of **30 words**. First names of people **do not count**. Be sure that you satisfy the purpose of the task. The structure or expressions used should be connected logically and should demonstrate a wide range of vocabulary.

Topic B: You have been asked to get some information from the new student from a country where the language you are studying is spoken. Write him/her a short note to ask questions about the new student in the *target language*. You may wish to include questions about:

- ♦ His/her name
- ♦ Where he/she lives
- ♦ What he/she likes to do
- ♦ Age and date of birth

_____

_____

_____

_____

_____

_____

_____

Family Life Writing Tasks

In the spaces provided, complete the following writing task. This writing task should be written entirely in the **target language** and should contain a minimum of **30 words**. First names of people **do not count**. Be sure that you satisfy the purpose of the task. The structure or expressions used should be connected logically and should demonstrate a wide range of vocabulary.

Topic A: You are planning a trip for the summer to a country where the language you are studying is spoken. Write a note to the tour guide describing your family in the *target language*. You may wish to include the following ideas:

- ♦ Identify the members of your family
- ♦ Tell the number of people in your family
- ♦ Describe some activities your family does together
- ♦ Describe the physical appearance of family members

Family Life Writing Tasks

In the spaces provided, complete the following writing task. This writing task should be written entirely in the **target language** and should contain a minimum of **30 words**. First names of people **do not count**. Be sure that you satisfy the purpose of the task. The structure or expressions used should be connected logically and should demonstrate a wide range of vocabulary.

Topic B: Your friend would like to meet your cousin. Write a note in the *target language* to your friend describing your cousin. You may wish to include:

- ◆ Your cousin's name and age
- ◆ His/her personality
- ◆ His/her physical appearance
- ◆ Activities for them to do together

_____

_____

_____

_____

_____

_____

_____

House and Home Writing Tasks

In the spaces provided, complete the following writing task. This writing task should be written entirely in the **target language** and should contain a minimum of **30 words**. First names of people **do not count**. Be sure that you satisfy the purpose of the task. The structure or expressions used should be connected logically and should demonstrate a wide range of vocabulary.

Topic A: Write a short note in the *target language* to your pen pal in a country where the language you are studying is spoken. Describe why you like your new house. You may wish to include:

- The size of the house or apartment
- The names of the rooms
- The furniture
- The garden

_____

_____

_____

_____

_____

_____

_____

_____

House and Home Writing Tasks

In the spaces provided, complete the following writing task. This writing task should be written entirely in the **target language** and should contain a minimum of **30 words**. First names of people **do not count**. Be sure that you satisfy the purpose of the task. The structure or expressions used should be connected logically and should demonstrate a wide range of vocabulary.

Topic B: You and your family are going to exchange houses with a family where the language you are studying is spoken. Write a note to describe your bedroom in the *target language*. You may wish to include the following ideas:

- ◆ The color of your room
- ◆ What activities you do in that room
- ◆ The items you have in your room
- ◆ How you feel about it

_____

_____

_____

_____

_____

_____

_____

Education Writing Tasks

In the spaces provided, complete the following writing task. This writing task should be written entirely in the **target language** and should contain a minimum of **30 words**. First names of people **do not count**. Be sure that you satisfy the purpose of the task. The structure or expressions used should be connected logically and should demonstrate a wide range of vocabulary.

Topic A: Write a note in the *target language* to a pen pal in a country where the language you are studying is spoken. Tell him/her about one of your classes in school You may wish to include:

- ♦ The subject
- ♦ Activities you do in class
- ♦ How you feel about the class
- ♦ The materials you have for the class

Education Writing Tasks

In the spaces provided, complete the following writing task. This writing task should be written entirely in the **target language** and should contain a minimum of **30 words**. First names of people **do not count**. Be sure that you satisfy the purpose of the task. The structure or expressions used should be connected logically and should demonstrate a wide range of vocabulary.

Topic B: A student from a country where the language you are studying is spoken will be attending your school later this year. Write a note in the *target language* to him/her to describe your school. You may wish to include the following ideas:

- The classes that are offered
- The activities that are available
- Information about the students
- Information about the teachers

_____

_____

_____

_____

_____

_____

_____

Community and Neighborhood Writing Tasks

In the spaces provided, complete the following writing task. This writing task should be written entirely in the **target language** and should contain a minimum of **30 words**. First names of people **do not count**. Be sure that you satisfy the purpose of the task. The structure or expressions used should be connected logically and should demonstrate a wide range of vocabulary.

Topic A: For your birthday your relatives have sent you a plane ticket to a little town in a country where the language you are studying is spoken. Write a note in the *target language* to your best friend telling him/her about the town and what you do there. You may wish to include the following ideas:

- ♦ Where it is located
- ♦ What the town is like
- ♦ What activities you do there
- ♦ Different places to go for entertainment

_____

_____

_____

_____

_____

_____

_____

Community and Neighborhood Writing Tasks

In the spaces provided, complete the following writing task. This writing task should be written entirely in the **target language** and should contain a minimum of **30 words**. First names of people **do not count**. Be sure that you satisfy the purpose of the task. The structure or expressions used should be connected logically and should demonstrate a wide range of vocabulary.

Topic B: Write a note in the *target language* to your pen pal telling him/her about one of your favorite places in your town. You may wish to include the following ideas:

- The name and description of the place
- Who is with you
- Why you go there
- When you go there

_____

_____

_____

_____

_____

_____

_____

Meal Taking Writing Tasks

In the spaces provided, complete the following writing task. This writing task should be written entirely in the **target language** and should contain a minimum of **30 words**. First names of people **do not count**. Be sure that you satisfy the purpose of the task. The structure or expressions used should be connected logically and should demonstrate a wide range of vocabulary.

Topic A: You are staying with a family in the country where the language you are studying is spoken. You are planning a surprise birthday party for your host mother. Write a journal entry in the *target language* about your plans for the party. You may wish to include the following ideas:

- ♦ Main course items, beverages and dessert
- ♦ When the party will take place
- ♦ Who is invited
- ♦ Who will cook, serve and clean-up

_____

_____

_____

_____

_____

_____

Meal Taking Writing Tasks

In the spaces provided, complete the following writing task. This writing task should be written entirely in the **target language** and should contain a minimum of **30 words**. First names of people **do not count**. Be sure that you satisfy the purpose of the task. The structure or expressions used should be connected logically and should demonstrate a wide range of vocabulary.

Topic B: You are staying in a country where the language you are studying is spoken. Write a note in the *target language* to a friend inviting him/her to a restaurant for dinner. You may include:

- ♦ The invitation to the restaurant
- ♦ Suggestions for the type of restaurant
- ♦ When you are going to meet
- ♦ Where you are going to meet

_____

_____

_____

_____

_____

_____

_____

Shopping Writing Tasks

In the spaces provided, complete the following writing task. This writing task should be written entirely in the **target language** and should contain a minimum of **30 words**. First names of people **do not count**. Be sure that you satisfy the purpose of the task. The structure or expressions used should be connected logically and should demonstrate a wide range of vocabulary.

Topic A: You are staying with a family in a country where the language you are studying is spoken. You are planning to go shopping. Write a journal entry in the *target language* about your plans. You may wish to include:

- ◆ When you are going
- ◆ The stores you are going to
- ◆ How you are going there
- ◆ The items you are going to buy

_____

_____

_____

_____

_____

_____

_____

Shopping Writing Tasks

In the spaces provided, complete the following writing task. This writing task should be written entirely in the **target language** and should contain a minimum of **30 words**. First names of people **do not count**. Be sure that you satisfy the purpose of the task. The structure or expressions used should be connected logically and should demonstrate a wide range of vocabulary.

Topic B: You are staying with a host family. Write a thank-you note in the *target language* to your host mother for a birthday gift that she bought you. You may wish to include the following ideas:

- Identify the gift
- Describe the gift
- Tell why you like it
- Explain when you are going to use it

_____

_____

_____

_____

_____

_____

_____

Health and Welfare Writing Tasks

In the spaces provided, complete the following writing task. This writing task should be written entirely in the **target language** and should contain a minimum of **30 words**. First names of people **do not count**. Be sure that you satisfy the purpose of the task. The structure or expressions used should be connected logically and should demonstrate a wide range of vocabulary.

Topic A: You become ill while on vacation. Write a note in the *target language* to your cousin about your illness. You may wish to include the following ideas:

- ◆ Identify the illness
- ◆ Describe the symptoms
- ◆ A remedy you are trying
- ◆ Tell if you are going to the doctor

_____

_____

_____

_____

_____

_____

_____

Health and Welfare Writing Tasks

In the spaces provided, complete the following writing task. This writing task should be written entirely in the **target language** and should contain a minimum of **30 words**. First names of people **do not count**. Be sure that you satisfy the purpose of the task. The structure or expressions used should be connected logically and should demonstrate a wide range of vocabulary.

Topic B: You and your family are on vacation in a country where the language you are studying is spoken. You suddenly see an extraterrestrial–being during your travels. Write a note in the *target language* to the local newspaper describing the being. You may wish to include these ideas:

- A description for its face
- The number of arms and legs
- Its size
- Your opinion of it

_____

_____

_____

_____

_____

_____

Physical Environment Writing Tasks

In the spaces provided, complete the following writing task. This writing task should be written entirely in the **target language** and should contain a minimum of **30 words**. First names of people **do not count**. Be sure that you satisfy the purpose of the task. The structure or expressions used should be connected logically and should demonstrate a wide range of vocabulary.

Topic A: Your family has decided to move. Write a journal entry in the *target language* about the type of area to which you would like to move. You may wish to include:

- The geography of the area
- Why you like that area
- Activities to do in that area
- Your feelings about that area

_____

_____

_____

_____

_____

_____

_____

Physical Environment Writing Tasks

In the spaces provided, complete the following writing task. This writing task should be written entirely in the **target language** and should contain a minimum of **30 words**. First names of people **do not count**. Be sure that you satisfy the purpose of the task. The structure or expressions used should be connected logically and should demonstrate a wide range of vocabulary.

Topic B: You are spending a week during the summer at your aunt's farm. Write a note in the *target language* to your friend back home telling about this experience. You may wish to include:

- The geography of the area
- Animals on the farm
- The fruits and vegetables your aunt sells
- When you are arriving home

_____

_____

_____

_____

_____

_____

_____

Earning a Living Writing Tasks

In the spaces provided, complete the following writing task. This writing task should be written entirely in the **target language** and should contain a minimum of **30 words**. First names of people **do not count**. Be sure that you satisfy the purpose of the task. The structure or expressions used should be connected logically and should demonstrate a wide range of vocabulary.

Topic A: You have just seen an ad in an international newspaper for the job of your dreams. Write a letter in the *target language* applying for this job. You may wish to include:

- ♦ Why you would like the job
- ♦ Your qualifications
- ♦ When you can begin
- ♦ Questions you have about the job

Earning a Living Writing Tasks

In the spaces provided, complete the following writing task. This writing task should be written entirely in the **target language** and should contain a minimum of **30 words**. First names of people **do not count**. Be sure that you satisfy the purpose of the task. The structure or expressions used should be connected logically and should demonstrate a wide range of vocabulary.

Topic B: You have a summer job. Write a note in the *target language* to your pen pal telling him/her about your job. You may wish to include:

- ◆ Where you work
- ◆ A description of your job
- ◆ Your hours
- ◆ Your feelings about your job

_____

_____

_____

_____

_____

_____

_____

Leisure Writing Tasks

In the spaces provided, complete the following writing task. This writing task should be written entirely in the **target language** and should contain a minimum of **30 words**. First names of people **do not count**. Be sure that you satisfy the purpose of the task. The structure or expressions used should be connected logically and should demonstrate a wide range of vocabulary.

Topic A: In a note in the *target language* to your pen pal, tell him/her about a television show you like. You may wish to include:

- ♦   When you watch the show
- ♦   Where you watch it
- ♦   The characters or performers in the show
- ♦   Your feelings about the show

_____

_____

_____

_____

_____

_____

_____

Leisure Writing Tasks

In the spaces provided, complete the following writing task. This writing task should be written entirely in the **target language** and should contain a minimum of **30 words**. First names of people **do not count**. Be sure that you satisfy the purpose of the task. The structure or expressions used should be connected logically and should demonstrate a wide range of vocabulary.

Topic B: You attend a sports event while on vacation. Write a note in the *target language* to your foreign language teacher about this experience. You may wish to include:

- ◆ The event(s) you are watching
- ◆ Your favorite player or team
- ◆ Who is with you
- ◆ What other leisure activities you will do later

_____

_____

_____

_____

_____

_____

_____

Public and Private Services Writing Tasks

In the spaces provided, complete the following writing task. This writing task should be written entirely in the **target language** and should contain a minimum of **30 words**. First names of people **do not count**. Be sure that you satisfy the purpose of the task. The structure or expressions used should be connected logically and should demonstrate a wide range of vocabulary.

Topic A: Your family has hired a house sitter to take care of your house while you go on vacation. The house sitter speaks the language you are studying. Your parents have asked you to write a note in the *target language* telling the sitter how to handle messages. You may wish to include:

- When the mail arrives
- To write the telephone callers' names and numbers on paper
- What to do in case of an emergency
- How to reach you

_____

_____

_____

_____

_____

_____

_____

Public and Private Services Writing Tasks

In the spaces provided, complete the following writing task. This writing task should be written entirely in the **target language** and should contain a minimum of **30 words**. First names of people **do not count**. Be sure that you satisfy the purpose of the task. The structure or expressions used should be connected logically and should demonstrate a wide range of vocabulary.

Topic B: You are studying for a year in a foreign country. You would like to send some items back home to your family. Write a note in the *target language* to your host mother asking her to go to the post office for you. You may wish to include:

- ♦ A request to go to the post office
- ♦ What you want to send
- ♦ How you want to send the package
- ♦ Questions about the cost

Travel Writing Tasks

In the spaces provided, complete the following writing task. This writing task should be written entirely in the **target language** and should contain a minimum of **30 words**. First names of people **do not count**. Be sure that you satisfy the purpose of the task. The structure or expressions used should be connected logically and should demonstrate a wide range of vocabulary.

Topic A: Your family is traveling to a foreign country and your parents ask you to write a note, in the *target language*, making the hotel arrangements. You may wish to include:

- ♦ The number of persons
- ♦ The dates of the trip
- ♦ The type of room you would like
- ♦ Questions about the hotel, price of room, etc.

_____

_____

_____

_____

_____

_____

_____

Travel Writing Tasks

In the spaces provided, complete the following writing task. This writing task should be written entirely in the **target language** and should contain a minimum of **30 words**. First names of people **do not count**. Be sure that you satisfy the purpose of the task. The structure or expressions used should be connected logically and should demonstrate a wide range of vocabulary.

Topic B: You are planning to take a trip this summer to a country where your target language is spoken. Write a journal entry in the *target language* about your plans. You may wish to include:

- A description of the place(s) you would like to visit
- The activities you are going to do there
- How you are traveling
- When you are going to return

_____

_____

_____

_____

_____

_____

_____

Grading Criteria
for Writing Tasks

Student Name: _____

Writing Checklist

Please refer to the full writing rubric for definitions of each level.

	4	3	2	1	0
Purpose/Task • Satisfies the task • Connects ideas to task/purpose • Exhibits a logical and coherent sequence of ideas					
Vocabulary • Incorporates a range of nouns, verbs, and/or adjectives as appropriate to task • Uses relevant and accurate words					
Structure/Conventions • Subject/verb agreement • Noun/adjective agreement • Correct word order • Spelling					
Word Count • Comprehensible • In target language • Contributes to the development of the task	30+	25-29	20–24	15–19	<15

Total Raw Score _____

Converted Score _____

Part 4 Conversion Chart					
Total Raw Score	14–16	11–13	8–10	5–7	2–4	0–1
Total Credits	5	4	3	2	1	0

◆ Note that a zero can be given in any of the dimensions when a student's performance falls below the criteria described for the performance level of 1.

◆ If a student's response receives a zero in the dimension of purpose/task, the student should receive no credit for that question. Please keep in mind, however, that students may employ a wide array of strategies to accomplish the purpose of the writing task, using a variety of vocabulary and grammatical structures.

Student Name:_____   **Detailed Writing Rubric**

Dimension	Student Performance Levels			
	4	**3**	**2**	**1**
Purpose/Task	Satisfies the task, connects all ideas to task/purpose, and exhibits a logical and coherent sequence of ideas throughout.	Satisfies the task, connections are implied, with few irrelevancies.	Satisfies the task, connections may be unclear, with some irrelevancies.	Makes at least one statement that satisfies the task. Remaining statements are irrelevant to the task.
Vocabulary	Uses a wide variety of vocabulary that expands the topic in the statement/question to include nouns, verbs, and/or adjectives, as appropriate to the task.	Uses a wide variety of vocabulary relevant to the topic in the statement /question to include nouns, verbs, and/or adjectives, as appropriate to the task.	Uses vocabulary, some of which is inaccurate or irrelevant to the task.	Uses limited vocabulary, most of which is inaccurate or irrelevant to the task.
Structure/ Conventions	Exhibits a high degree of control of structure/ conventions: · subject/verb agreement · noun/adjective agreement · correct word order · spelling Errors *do not* hinder overall comprehensibility of the passage.	Exhibits some control of structure/conventions: · subject/verb agreement · noun/adjective agreement · correct word order · spelling Errors *do not* hinder overall comprehensibility of the passage.	Exhibits some control of structure/conventions: · subject/verb agreement · noun/adjective agreement · correct word order · spelling Errors *do* hinder overall comprehensibility of the passage.	Demonstrates little control of structure or convention, or errors impede overall comprehensibility of the passage.
Word Count	Uses 30 or more comprehensible words in target language that contribute to the development of the task.	Uses 25–29 comprehensible words in target language that contribute to the development of the task.	Uses 20–24 comprehensible words in target language that contribute to the development of the task.	Uses 15–19 comprehensible words in target language that contribute to the development of the task.
			Total Raw Score	
			Total Score*	

♦ Note that a zero can be given in any of the dimensions when a student's performance falls below the criteria described for the performance level of 1. If a student's response receives a zero in the dimension of *purpose/task*, the student should receive no credit for that question.

Part 4 Conversion Chart					
Total Raw Score	14–16	11–13	8–10	5–7	2–4	0–1
Total Credits	5	4	3	2	1	0

Word-Count Guidelines

> **Definition**: A word is a letter or collection of letters, surrounded by space, that in the target language is comprehensible and that contributes to the development of the task. This definition applies even when words are grammatically incorrect.
> <u>Examples</u>: "à le" (French) counts as 2 words; "de el" (Spanish) counts as two words.

- Numbers, unless written as words, and names of people are *not* included in the word count.
- Place names and brand names from the target culture count as one word; all other places (*K-Mart*) and brand names (*Pepsi, Coke*) are disregarded.
- Contractions count as one word.
- The salutations and closings of notes written in the target language are counted. [There is no penalty if students do not use salutations or closings.]
- Commonly used abbreviations in the target language are counted.

Examples and Word Counts

English Example	Word Count	French Example	Word Count	German Example	Word Count	Italian Example	Word Count	Spanish Example	Word Count
New York City	0	Île St. Louis	3	Auf Wiedersehen	2	Guiseppe	0	Nueva York	2
		La Tour Eiffel	3	Wie geht's	2	Il Colosseo	2	el Corte Inglés	3
		La Eiffel Tower	2	Deutschland	1	Venezia	1	La Universidad de Salamanca	4
		Paris	1	München	1	nell'aula	1	José	0
		L'hôpital	1	Markplatz	1	la *Coca-Cola*	1	La Torre Pendente	3
		Jacques	0	*Fanta*	1	fare lo shopping	3		
		des Ètats-Unis	2	*Sprite*	0	all'una	1		
		les Galleries Lafayettes	3			alle tre	2		
		J'ai	1			d'estate	1		
						in prima-vera	2		

Grading Criteria for
Informal and Formal Speaking

HOW TO USE THE INFORMAL SPEAKING RUBRIC

Part 1a: Informal Classroom Evaluation (as currently administered)

Scores for Part 1a of the examination are based on students performance in daily classroom activities during the designated assessment period. This assessment presumes that instruction routinely includes frequent opportunities for students to engage in a variety of realistic oral communications. These communications must be consistent with functions, topics, and situations for listening/speaking outcomes at Checkpoint A in the State syllabus. **Reading aloud and recitation or memorized text do not constitute oral communication for the purpose of this assessment.**

Presently, the criterion for this assessment is frequency/consistency: how often students express themselves in a manner consistent with the speaking proficiency level for Checkpoint A in the State syllabus. Scores must be expressed in whole numbers according to the following table: All the time: 10; Most of the time: 7-9; Half of the time: 4-6; Seldom: 1-3; Never: 0.

Features of the Rubric:

- The rubric describes a continuum of performances from Level 4 (most proficient) to Level 1 (least proficient).
- There are six criteria (called dimensions) in the informal speaking rubric: initiation; response; conversational strategies; vocabulary; structure; and cultural appropriateness.
- The dimensions are articulated in the left column of the rubric.
- Explanation and examples of terms are attached.
- The rubric is presented in two forms. The Informal Speaking Rubric describes the characteristics of a performance at each level. The Informal Speaking Checklist is simply another format of the same information. Scorers who prefer the checklist should refer to the Informal Speaking Rubric for definitions at each level.

Applying the Dimensions:

- Scores are determined by matching evidence from exchanges with students to the language of the rubric.
- Students are assigned a score for their performance in informal speaking on each of the six dimensions.
- The raw scores for each dimension represent the extent to which the student exhibits proficiency on that dimension; that is to say, the individual scores recognize a student's strength in the areas of initiation, response, conversational strategies, vocabulary, structure, and cultural appropriateness.
- The scores for each dimension are then added to determine a total raw score.
- The raw score is converted to a score ranging from 0 to 10 points, using the chart provided on each rubric.

Adapted from The New York State Standards

Student Name _____ **Total Raw Score** _____ **Total Score** _____

Part IA: Detailed Informal Speaking Rubric

Dimension	4	3	2	1
Initiation	Eagerly initiates speech, utilizing appropriate attention getting devices. Easily asks questions and speaks spontaneously.	Is willing to initiate speech, utilizing appropriate attention-getting devices. Asks questions and speaks evenly.	Sometimes initiates speech, using attention-getting devices. Sometimes asks questions and speaks hesitantly.	Is reluctant to initiate speech and struggles to ask questions. Speech is halting.
Response	Almost always responds appropriately to questions/statements.	Frequently responds appropriately to questions/statements.	Sometimes responds appropriately to questions/statements.	Rarely responds appropriately to questions/statements.
Conversational Strategies	Clarifies and continues conversation, using all or some of the following strategies: • circumlocution • survival strategies • intonation • self-correction • verbal cues	Uses all or some strategies, but may need occasional prompting.	Uses some strategies and needs frequent prompting to further the conversation.	Uses few strategies. Relies heavily on conversation partner to sustain conversation. Rarely responds even with frequent prompting.
Vocabulary	• Incorporates a variety of old and new vocabulary. • Uses idiomatic expressions appropriate to topic. • Speaks clearly and imitates accurate pronunciation.	• Utilizes a variety of old and limited new vocabulary. • Attempts to use idiomatic expressions appropriate to topic. • Speaks clearly and attempts accurate pronunciation.	• Relies on basic vocabulary. • Speech is comprehensible in spite of mispronunciations.	• Uses limited vocabulary. • Mispronunciations impede comprehensibility.
Structure	Makes few errors in the following areas: • verbs in utterances when necessary with appropriate subject/verb agreement • noun and adjective agreement • correct word order and article adjectives Errors do not hinder comprehensibility.	Makes several errors in structure which do not affect overall comprehensibility.	Makes several errors which may interfere with comprehensibility.	Makes utterances which are so brief that there is little evidence of structure and comprehensibility is impeded.
Cultural Appropriateness	Almost always uses/interprets cultural manifestations when appropriate to the task (e.g., greeting, leave taking, gestures, proximity, etc.).	Frequently uses/interprets cultural manifestations when appropriate to the task.	Sometimes uses/interprets cultural manifestations when appropriate to the task.	Rarely uses/interprets cultural manifestations when appropriate to the task.

◆ A zero can be given in any of the above dimensions when the student's performance falls below the criteria described for "1".

Part 1A Conversion Chart										
Total Raw Score	22-24	19-21	17-18	14-16	12-13	10-11	7-9	5-6	3-4	1-2
Total Informal Speaking Score	10	9	8	7	6	5	4	3	2	1

Adapted from The New York State Standards

EXPLANATIONS, DEFINITIONS, AND EXAMPLES
Part 1A: Informal Speaking

Conversational Strategies: ways to clarify and continue a conversation. Student will use all or some, as appropriate to conversation.

CIRCUMLOCUTION
♦ Uses familiar vocabulary and structures to express meaning beyond his/her current level of knowledge.
   Example: tiger (a big cat with stripes in the zoo)

SURVIVAL SKILLS
♦ Uses learned expressions in appropriate situations to sustain conversation.
   Examples: please explain, please repeat, how do you say, I don t understand

♦ Uses nonverbal cues to clarify meaning.
   Examples: facial expression, body language

INTONATION
♦ Uses language-appropriate inflection to indicate purpose of utterance.
   Example: rising pitch to show question

SELF-CORRECTION
♦ Uses self-correction to clarify meaning.
   Example: You go ... no, *I* go

RESPONDS TO VERBAL CUES
♦ Uses utterances of conversation partner as a clue or resource for unfamiliar vocabulary and structures to use in his/her own utterances, to self-correct, clarify, or restate.
   Example: A - Give me a thing to write with.
                    B - OK. Do you want a pen or a pencil?
                    A - I need a pencil.

ATTENTION-GETTING DEVICES
♦ Uses strategies to initiate a conversation.
   Example: A - Hello!
                    B - Excuse me.
                    C - Good morning.

Adapted from The New York State Standards

Student Name: _____

Part 1A: Informal Speaking Checklist

Please refer to the full writing rubric for definitions of each level.

	4	3	2	1	0
Initiation ♦ Initiates speech and asks questions ♦ Uses appropriate attention-getting devices ♦ Speaks spontaneously					
Response ♦ Responds appropriately to questions/statements					
Conversational Strategies to Clarify and Continue Conversations Using: ♦ Circumlocution ♦ Survival strategies ♦ Intonation ♦ Self-correction ♦ Verbal cues					
Vocabulary ♦ Incorporates variety of old and new vocabulary ♦ Uses idiomatic expressions appropriate to topic ♦ Speaks clearly and imitates accurate pronunciation					
Structure ♦ Uses verbs in utterances when necessary with appropriate subject/verb agreement ♦ Makes nouns and adjectives agree ♦ Uses correct word order and article adjectives					
Cultural Appropriateness ♦ Uses/interprets cultural manifestations appropriate to the task (e.g., greeting, leave taking, gestures, proximity, etc.)					

Total Raw Score ☐
Total Informal Speaking Score ☐

♦ A zero can be given in any of the above dimensions when the student's performance falls below the criteria described for "1".

Part 1A Conversion Chart									
Total Raw Score	22-24	19-21	17-18	14-16	12-13	10-11	7-9	5-6	3-4	1-2
Total Informal Speaking Score	10	9	8	7	6	5	4	3	2	1

SCORING THE FORMAL SPEAKING TASKS
Part 1B

As the rater of the formal speaking task, the teacher gives a maximum of <u>five</u> credits for each task according to the following criteria:

- **One credit** *for each of the four student utterances that is comprehensible and appropriate.*
  (Comprehensibility means that the utterance would make sense to native speakers who know no English but are used to foreigners trying to speak their language. Appropriateness means that the utterance contributes to the completion of the task.)

- **One credit** for the quality of all four comprehensible and appropriate student utterances.
  (Quality means overall spontaneity, fluency, and accuracy *within the scope of the Checkpoint A proficiency statement in the State syllabus.*)

As the conversation partner and rater, the teacher may make two attempts at eliciting each of the four student utterances. If the student produces no comprehensible and appropriate utterance after the teacher's first two eliciting attempts at the very beginning of the conversation, the student receives no credit for the entire task. However, during the conversation, if a student produces no comprehensible and appropriate utterance after the teacher's second eliciting attempt, the student receives no credit for that utterance, and the teacher shifts to another aspect of the task.

To facilitate rating while acting as the conversation partner, the teacher should use a score sheet to keep track of the student's comprehensible and appropriate utterances, to record the number of eliciting attempts for each, and to determine whether the quality credit is warranted. A sample score sheet is provided on page 92. Certain teacher-student interactions, although natural in the course of a conversation, do not provide evidence of the student's ability to produce language. They should be disregarded for rating purposes. Examples of such interactions include:

- yes-no responses
- restatements of all or essential parts of what the teacher has said
- proper names used in isolation
- socializing devices (Hello, How are you, etc.) *except* in socializing tasks when appropriate.

Adapted from The New York State Standards

QUALITY POINT GUIDELINES
Part 1B: Formal Speaking

For each task, students who require three or more second attempts **do not** qualify for the quality point (i.e., a student with three or more checkmarks in the second column of the scoring sheet is not eligible for the quality point).

Responses eligible for a quality point contain evidence from each of the following categories as appropriate to Checkpoint A:
FLUENCY, COMPLEXITY, and ACCURACY.

FLUENCY may be demonstrated by, but not limited to, ability to sustain the conversation, spontaneity, efficiency of task completion, intonation, pronunciation, and exclusive use of target language.

COMPLEXITY may be demonstrated by, but not limited to, ability to initiate/direct conversation, risk taking, creativity, choice and variety of vocabulary, and grammatical structures.

ACCURACY may be demonstrated by, but not limited to, correct grammatical structure, use of self-correction strategies, and cultural appropriateness.

Adapted from The New York State Standards

SECOND LANGUAGE PROFICIENCY EXAMINATIONS MODERN LANGUAGES
Sample Score Sheet for Part 1B: Formal Speaking Test

Student's Name: _____

	Utterance		First Attempt	Second Attempt	
Task: A _____ (Task No.*)	1.	(____*)	_____	_____	
	2.		_____	_____	
	3.		_____	_____	
	4.		_____	_____	Quality: _____
					Total: _____
Task: B _____ (Task No.)	1.	(____*)	_____	_____	
	2.		_____	_____	
	3.		_____	_____	
	4.		_____	_____	Quality: _____
					Total: _____
Task: C _____ (Task No.)	1.	(____*)	_____	_____	
	2.		_____	_____	
	3.		_____	_____	
	4.		_____	_____	Quality: _____
					Total: _____
Task: D _____ (Task No.)	1.	(____*)	_____	_____	
	2.		_____	_____	
	3.		_____	_____	
	4.		_____	_____	Quality: _____
					Total: _____

* When completing the formal scoring sheet, write the task number in the space provided. Check off in the parenthesis when the student initiates the conversation .

New York State Standards

NEW YORK STATE STANDARD 1: <u>Communication Skills</u>
Checkpoint A: Modern Languages (LOTE)

Students will be able to use a language other than English for communication

Key Idea 1: **LISTENING & SPEAKING** are primary communicative goals in modern language learning. These skills are used for the purposes of *socializing, providing and acquiring information, expressing personal feelings and opinions, and getting others to adopt a course of action.*

<u>Performance Indicators:</u> **Students will:**

- comprehend language consisting of simple vocabulary and structures in face-to-face conversation with peers and familiar adults
- comprehend the main idea of more extended conversations with some unfamiliar vocabulary and structures as well as cognates of English words
- call upon repetition, rephrasing, and nonverbal cues to derive or convey meaning from a language other than English
- use appropriate strategies to initiate and engage in simple conversations with more fluent or native speakers of the same age group, familiar adults, and providers of common public services

This is evident, for example, when students:

- exchange simple greetings and answer questions about self and family
- listen to radio broadcasts and answer questions about main ideas
- speak in complete sentences, using present tense and, occasionally, markers for past and future tense
- ask for information and directions
- discuss classroom activities with a peer
- use appropriate body language and gestures to supplement the spoken word.

Key Idea 2: **READING & WRITING** are used in languages other than English for the purposes of socializing, providing and acquiring information, expressing personal feelings and opinions, and getting others to adopt a course of action.

<u>Performance Indicators:</u> **Students will:**

- understand the main idea and some details of simple informative materials written for native speakers
- compose short, informal notes and messages to exchange information with members of the target culture

92

This is evident, for example, when students:

- Obtain information from materials written in the target language including short notes, brief messages, posters, printed advertisements, illustrated simple texts from newspapers and magazines
- Guess the meaning of more complex written material, using context, recognition of cognates, accompanying illustrations, and prior knowledge of situations and issues
- Write a brief message about an everyday activity, using simple sentence structure, not necessarily limited to present tense.

NEW YORK STATE 2: Cultural Understanding
Checkpoint A: Modern Languages (LOTE)

Students will develop cross-cultural skills and understandings

---

Key Idea: **EFFECTIVE COMMUNICATION** involves meanings that go beyond words and require an understanding of perceptions, gestures, folklore, and family and community dynamics. All of these elements can affect whether and how well a message is received.

Performance Indicators: **Students will:**

- use some key cultural traits of the societies in which the target language is spoken

This is evident, for example, when students:

- Recognize cultural patterns and traditions of target cultures in the target language
- Understand the cultural implications of the spoken language and of the dynamics of social interaction
- Correctly use and interpret cultural manifestations, such as gestures accompanying greeting and leave taking and the appropriate distance to maintain.

FUNCTIONS

Socializing:
- greeting
- leave-taking
- introducing
- thanking
- apologizing

Providing and obtaining information about:
- facts
- events
- needs
- opinions
- attitudes
- feelings

Expressing personal feelings about:
- facts
- events
- opinions
- attitudes

Getting others to adopt a course of action by:
- suggesting
- requesting
- directing
- advising
- warning
- convincing
- praising

SITUATIONS

LISTENING:
Information and announcements from providers of common public services in face-to-face communications
Information (bulletins/announcements) provided over loudspeakers, radio, and television
LISTENING/SPEAKING:
Interaction with providers of common public services in face-to-face communications
Informal everyday conversations with individual peers and adults
Informal conversations with peers and familiar adults

READING:
Information provided to the general public on forms, signs, billboards, posters, labels, programs, timetables, maps, plans, menus, etc.
Announcements, ads, and short reports of general interest in newspapers, magazines, and other publications; short, informal notes
WRITING:
Forms to be filled out for the use of common public services
Informal notes for communications in everyday life situations

This section adapted from The New York State Standards and The New York State Syllabus

TOPICS

PERSONAL IDENTIFICATION: age, nationality, address and telephone number, family, occupation, place and date of birth, height, weight, complexion, facial features, body shape, color of hair/eyes, disabilities, character, personality, likes and dislikes, tastes and interests

HOUSE AND HOME: house, apartment, identification, size/function, furnishings, garden/terrace/balcony

FAMILY LIFE: family members, activities

COMMUNITY/NEIGHBORHOOD: common activities, local stores/facilities, recreational opportunities

PHYSICAL ENVIRONMENT: big city, small town, village, suburb, country, geography of area, seasons, temperature/precipitation/wind, opportunities for recreation and entertainment

MEAL TAKING/FOOD/DRINK: everyday family fare, regional and national specialties, fast food, food and drink preparation, regular family meals, eating with friends/relatives, eating out

HEALTH AND WELFARE: parts of the body: identification, symptoms of illness

EDUCATION: types of schools, subjects, schedule/school year, extracurricular activities

EARNING A LIVING: commonly known occupations

LEISURE: after school, weekends, holidays, vacations, hobbies/sports/other interests, use of media, religious events, traditions and customs, family occasions

PUBLIC AND PRIVATE SERVICES: telephone, mail, post office

SHOPPING: shopping centers, specialty shops, neighborhood merchants, department stores, markets; shopping patterns: time, currency, interaction with sales staff, staples and everyday purchases, prices

TRAVEL: means of transportation, maps, timetables and fares, signs and instructions, interaction at ticket counters, advertisements/promotional information

CURRENT EVENTS: miscellaneous news, arts (theater/cinema/ music), people in the arts, special events

PROFICIENCIES

LISTENING
Can comprehend simple statements and questions. Usually comprehends the main idea of longer but simple messages and conversations. Often requires repetition for comprehension even when listening to persons who are used to speaking with non-natives.

SPEAKING
Can initiate and respond to simple statements and engage in simple face-to-face conversation within the vocabulary, structure, and phonology appropriate to the communicative situations and functions at this level.

Can be understood, with some repetitions and circumlocutions, by native speakers used to foreigners attempting to speak their language.

READING
Can understand simple material for informative or social purposes. Can understand the essential content of short, general, public statements and standardized messages. Can comprehend the main ideas of materials containing simple structure and syntax when relying on visual cues and prior familiarity with the topic.

Understanding is limited to simple language containing only the highest frequency grammatical patterns and vocabulary items. Can sometimes guess at cognates and highly contextualized unfamiliar vocabulary. May have to read the material several times in order to achieve understanding.

WRITING
Can express basic personal needs and compose short messages on very familiar topics based on personal experience. Writing consists mostly of mastered vocabulary and structures in simple sentences and phrases. Although errors in spelling and grammar are frequent, writing can be understood by native speakers used to dealing with foreigners.

CULTURE
Has knowledge of some aspects of the second language culture and is aware of the existence of cultures other than his/her own. Is able to function in authentic, common, everyday situations but makes frequent cultural errors that impede communication even with native speakers accustomed to dealing with foreigners.

SITUATIONS

	A	B	C
LISTENING			
Information and announcements from providers of common public services in face-to-face communications	•	•	•
Information (bulletins/announcements) provided over loudspeakers, radio, and television	•	•	•
Short presentations of interest to the general public given in person, on radio, or on television		•	•
Songs, live and recorded			•
Feature programs on television, in the movies, and on the radio			•

	A	B	C
LISTENING/SPEAKING			
Interaction with providers of common public services* in face-to-face communications	•	•	•
Informal everyday conversations with individual peers and adults	•	•	•
Informal conversations with peers and familiar adults	•	•	•
Interaction with providers of common public services* by telephone		•	•
Group conversations among peers and familiar adults		•	•
Group discussions with peers		•	•
Informal presentations to groups of peers and familiar adults		•	•

	A	B	C
READING			
Information provided to the general public on forms, signs, billboards and posters, labels, programs, timetables, maps, plans, menus, etc.	•	•	•
Announcements, ads, and short reports of general interest in newspapers, magazines, and other publications; short, informal notes	•	•	•
Simple business correspondence and pamphlets		•	•
Facts, opinions, feelings, and attitudes in correspondence from acquaintances and friends (peers and adults)		•	•

*Sales personnel, bank tellers, ticket agents, police, hotel personnel, etc.

	A	B	C
Letters to the editor and feature articles from general-interest publications		•	•
Excerpts from poetry and prose for cultural appreciation		•	•

	A	B	C
WRITING			
Forms to be filled out for the use of common public services	•	•	•
Informal notes for communications in everyday life situations	•	•	•
Brief reports describing simple situations and sequences of events		•	•
Personal letters to acquaintances and friends (peers and adults)		•	•
Formal letters to agencies, institutions, and businesses on topics of personal needs		•	•
Short samples of expository or creative writing			•

Curriculum Essentials/ Scope and Sequence/ State

Adapted from The New York State Standards

TOPICS

1. PERSONAL IDENTIFICATION

	A	B	C
Biographical Information			
age	•	•	•
nationality	•	•	•
address and telephone number	•	•	•
family	•	•	•
occupation	•	•	•
place and date of birth	•	•	•
Physical Characteristics			
height	•	•	•
weight	•	•	•
complexion	•	•	•
facial features	•	•	•
body shape	•	•	•
color of hair/eyes	•	•	•
disabilities	•	•	•
Psychological Characteristics			
character	•	•	•
personality	•	•	•
likes and dislikes	•	•	•
tastes and interests	•	•	•

2. HOUSE AND HOME

	A	B	C
Types of Lodging			
house	•	•	•
apartment	•	•	•
rental/ownership		•	•
Rooms and Other Lodging Components	A	B	C
identification	•	•	•
size/function	•	•	•
furnishings	•	•	•
garden/terrace/balcony	•	•	•
appliances		•	•

3. SERVICES

	A	B	C
repairs		•	•
public utilities			•
deliveries			•

4. FAMILY LIFE	•	•	•
family members	•	•	•
activities		•	•
roles and responsibilities			•
rapport among family members			
5. COMMUNITY/NEIGHBORHOOD	•	•	•
common activities	•	•	•
local stores/facilities	•	•	•
recreational opportunities			•
responsibilities/expectations			•
rapport among members of the community			
6. PHYSICAL ENVIRONMENT			
Physical Features	•	•	•
big city	•	•	•
small town	•	•	•
village	•	•	•
suburb	•	•	•
country	•	•	•
geography of area			
Climate and Weather	•	•	•
seasons	•	•	•
temperature/precipitation/wind		•	•
natural catastrophes		•	•
flora and fauna			•
impact on human life			
Quality of Environment	•	•	•
opportunities for recreation and entertainment			•
ecology			•
economy			•
aesthetics			
7. MEAL TAKING/FOOD/DRINK			
Types of Food and Drink	•	•	•
everyday family fare	•	•	•
regional and national specialties	•	•	•
fast food	•	•	•
food and drink preparation		•	•
special occasion menus			
Mealtime Interaction	•	•	•
regular family meals	•	•	•
eating with friends/relatives	•	•	•
eating out			
socializing in public establishments			•

8. HEALTH AND WELFARE

	A	B	C
Parts of the Body			
identification	•	•	•
care		•	•
Illness and Accidents			
symptoms of illness	•	•	•
medical services/treatment		•	•
insurance/social services			•

9. EDUCATION

	A	B	C
Secondary School Organization			
types of schools	•	•	•
subjects	•	•	•
schedule/school year	•	•	•
programs		•	•
content		•	•
examinations/grading		•	•
diploma			•
students' organizations			•
School Life			
extracurricular activities	•	•	•
relationships among students		•	•
relationships between staff and students		•	•
discipline		•	•
roles/responsibilities/ expectations			•
Educational System			
structure			•
personnel			•
society's needs/expectations			•

10. EARNING A LIVING

	A	B	C
Types of Employment			
commonly known occupations	•	•	•
summer/part-time employment		•	•
volunteer work			•
Work Conditions			
preparation/training		•	•
work roles/responsibilities		•	•
remunerations/benefits		•	•
relations with colleagues and employer			•

	A	B	C
Major Issues in Employment			•
job market situation			•
new trends in employment			•
labor/management relations			

11. LEISURE

	A	B	C
Available Leisure Time	•	•	•
after school	•	•	•
weekends	•	•	•
holidays	•	•	•
vacations			
Activities	•	•	•
hobbies/sports/other interests	•	•	•
use of media		•	•
organizations and facilities		•	•
cultural resources			
Special Occasions	•	•	•
religious events	•	•	•
traditions and customs	•	•	•
family occasions			

12. PUBLIC AND PRIVATE SERVICES

	A	B	C
Communications	•	•	•
telephone	•	•	•
mail		•	•
telegram			
Government Agencies	•	•	•
post office		•	•
customs		•	•
police			•
embassies and consulates			
Finances		•	•
banks		•	•
currency exchange offices			

13. SHOPPING

	A	B	C
Shopping Facilities and Products	•	•	•
shopping centers	•	•	•
specialty shops	•	•	•
neighborhood merchants	•	•	•
department stores	•	•	•
markets		•	•
mail-order companies			

Shopping Patterns	A	B	C
time (opening hours. . .)	•	•	•
currency	•	•	•
interaction with sales staff	•	•	•
staples and everyday purchases	•	•	•
modes of payment		•	•
weights/measurements/sizes		•	•

Shoppers' Information	A	B	C
prices	•	•	•
advertisements		•	•
consumer publications			•
labels/information brochures/directions			•

14. TRAVEL

Transportation	A	B	C
means of transportation	•	•	•
maps	•	•	•
timetables and fares	•	•	•
signs and instructions	•	•	•
interaction at ticket counters	•	•	•
advertisements/promotional information	•	•	•
itinerary		•	•
interaction at travel agencies		•	•
travel information agencies			•

Lodging	A	B	C
youth hostels		•	•
camping/caravanning		•	•
hotels and pensions		•	•
private guest arrangements		•	•

Holiday Travel Patterns	A	B	C
destinations		•	•
activities		•	•

15. CURRENT EVENTS

	A	B	C
Political, Social, and Economic Aspects			
miscellaneous news	•	•	•
political parties		•	•
present governments		•	•
current political issues		•	•
current economic issues		•	•
general description of society		•	•
executive, legislative, and judicial			•
status of the economy			•
trends in the economy			•
social classes and their relations			•
social programs			•
current social issues			•
Cultural Aspects			
arts (theater/cinema/music)	•	•	•
people in the arts	•	•	•
special events	•	•	•
institutions/facilities		•	•
historical and artistic sites		•	•
folklore		•	•
trends			•
Relations between United States and Target Language Countries			
opportunities for exchange		•	•
influence of one country on another			•
cultural links			•
economic relations			•
governmental relations			•
individual perceptions			•

For more detail on functions, situations, and topics teachers may refer to the New York State Syllabi.

Curriculum Essentials/ Scope and Sequence/ State